LESBIAN AND GAY

FOSTER AND ADOPTIVE PARENTS

Recruiting, Assessing, and Supporting an

Untapped Resource for Children and Youth

Gerald P. Mallon

Child Welfare League of America
Washington, DC

CWLA Press is an imprint of the Child Welfare League of America. CWLA is the nation's oldest and largest membership-based child welfare organization. We are committed to engaging people everywhere in promoting the well-being of children, youth, and their families, and protecting every child from harm. All proceeds from the sale of this book support CWLA's programs in behalf of children and families.

CHILD WELFARE LEAGUE OF AMERICA, INC.

HEADQUARTERS

440 First Street, NW, Third Floor, Washington, DC 20001-2085

E-mail: books@cwla.org

CURRENT PRINTING (last digit)

10 9 8 7 6 5 4 3 2 1

Cover and text design by Jennifer Geanakos

Edited by Julie Gwin

Printed in the United States of America

ISBN-13: 978-1-58760-104-0

ISBN-10: 1-58760-104-4

Library of Congress Cataloging-in-Publication Data

Lesbian and gay foster and adoptive parents : recruiting, assessing, and supporting an untapped resource for children and youth / Gerald P. Mallon

p. cm.

Includes bibliographical references.

ISBN 1-58760-104-4 (alk. paper)

1. Gay adoption—United States. 2. Foster parents—United States. 3. Gay parents—United States. 4. Social work with gays. 5. Social work with lesbians. I. Title.

HV875.72.U6M34 2006

362.73'3086640973—dc22   2006016379

For GWB
Thank you for compelling me to write this book.

Contents

ACKNOWLEDGMENTS

The Child Welfare League of America is grateful for the assistance of Tom Sullivan with the Human Rights Campaign, Washington, DC; Chris Hampton with the American Civil Liberties Union's Lesbian, Gay, Bisexual, Transgender and AIDS Projects, New York; photographer, Gregory Barton, Washington, DC; and Author Gary Mallon in providing the pictures used in this book.

FOREWORD

THIS BOOK WAS BORN OUT OF MY OUTRAGE, both professional and personal, that lesbians and gay men have been systematically excluded from almost all discussions that have focused on recruiting, assessing, and supporting potential foster and adoptive parents for the more than 513,000 American children and youth in need of stable, permanent, and loving families. It is unconscionable, in my estimation, that some politicians and some child welfare professionals attempt to ban an entire group of potential foster parents and adopters from consideration based on their personal bias, misinformation, and moralistic stereotypes.

Although efforts during the past eight years to recruit and support foster and adoptive parents are admirable and have genuinely brought about an increase in loving and permanent homes for children and youth in need, these efforts, at least on a national level, have completely and systematically excluded lesbians and gay men from the process. This book is an attempt to correct that omission.

As debate over the issue of gay and lesbian adoption flares in several states, clear indications are that positive changes are also occurring. In the first months of 2006, we have gotten good news about changes in attitudes toward gay and lesbian adoption in four states:

- On April 17th, the Arizona state senate defeated a proposal called HB 2696, giving preference to married couples' applications and greatly restricting the ability of single people, straight as well as gay and lesbian, to adopt a child in Arizona (Kerr, 2006).

- New Hampshire, a state that in 1999 ended its ban on adoptions by gay and lesbian people, continues to grapple with the issue, but now it struggles openly and in the context of full disclosure (Timmins, 2006).

- In Indiana, a three-judge panel of the Court of Appeals of Indiana ruled on April 13th that the state's adoption law could be interpreted to allow unmarried couples, including same-sex partners, to jointly adopt a child. The ruling approved the adoption of a baby girl, resolving a dispute between the courts in Morgan and Marion Counties (Leonard, 2006).

- In New York, the Evan B. Donaldson Adoption Institute released a new report in late March that found no child-centered reason to prevent gays and lesbians from becoming adoptive parents, and recommended that agencies use them more extensively to provide permanent, loving homes for children living in state care across the country (Crary, 2006).

My role as Professor at the Hunter College School of Social Work in New York City and as Executive Director of the National Resource Center for Family-Centered Practice and Permanency Planning, has put me in touch with many federal, state, and tribal leaders in child welfare throughout the country, many of whom share my view that lesbians and gay men should not be excluded from the pool of potential parents for America's children and youth in need of families. These valuable associations and dialogues have provided for me a stimulating context for the planning, coordination, and completion of this book. The ideas, discussions, and principles presented in this text, however, are mine alone and do not represent the official position of the Children's Bureau or the U.S. Department of Health and Human Services, or of any state, nor did I use any funds from any grant in developing this book over the past several years.

I am grateful to my colleague Bridget Betts, who coauthored with me the British version of this book (Mallon & Betts, 2005), and to Shaila Shah at the British Association of Adoption and Fostering for having the wisdom and insight to publish that book. I was delighted to be a part of that project and proud of our colleagues in child welfare, the politicians in the United Kingdom, and even Her Royal Highness Queen Elizabeth II, for having the foresight to pass a national law that permits lesbians and gay men to openly and legally foster and adopt children and youth in need of loving and permanent homes. It is my hope that the United States will one day follow the path trod first by the United Kingdom.

I am very grateful to the Child Welfare League of America (CWLA) for agreeing to publish this book. I have sometimes been critical of what I have over the years perceived as their organizational ambivalence about this topic, but when all is said and done, their commitment to lesbian and gay issues in child welfare remains a strong one. I am especially appreciative of Eve Klein, the former

Director of CWLA Publications, for her support and assistance, and to Yelba Quinn who is currently at CWLA publications for her careful editing and assistance throughtout this project. My colleagues Ada White, Director of Adoption Services; Millicent Williams, Director of Foster Care Services; and Rob Woronoff, Director of Gay and Lesbian Services, are to be thanked as well for their support throughout the development of this project.

On a personal note, I am grateful to my partner, Mike Rendino, one of the most extraordinary parents whom I have ever known, for reminding me through his example every day that parenting is a privilege and not a right. During those days when I was most disturbed by what I saw happening in our country and in some meetings that I attended, I was reminded of why I felt so strongly about this issue, because I had the privilege of witnessing his untiring commitment to being a great parent. I have often wished that the young people with whom I worked in child welfare systems could have had the experience of having a parent as wonderful and loving as Mike. It is important to note that while I am running around the country talking about the importance of integrating family-centered practices and helping define what constitutes good parenting and competent adoption practices, Mike is at home doing it! I am deeply appreciative of him for all of the support he has given me and for the love and gentle care that he provides for our family on a daily basis.

Finally, I am thankful also to Terry Boggis, the Director of Centerkids, the Family Program of the Lesbian, Gay, Bisexual, and Transgender Center in New York. Terry has almost single-handedly provided competent guidance and wise counsel to thousands of lesbians and gay men who have been interested in pursuing parenting even in the very early days when they were not so sure that they would be permitted to do so. Terry's commitment to our lesbian, gay, bisexual, and transgender community is remarkable, and my own personal thanks to her is inestimable.

—*GPM*
April 20, 2006

CHAPTER 1

INTRODUCTION

LESBIAN AND GAY FOSTER AND ADOPTIVE PARENTS: Recruiting, Assessing, and Supporting an Untapped Resource for Children and Youth provides social work practitioners with guidelines for working with lesbian and gay people interested in fostering or adopting. In contrast to their heterosexual counterparts, many lesbians and gay men view adoption and fostering as a first choice in considering parenthood, but for many reasons, by some, they have been regarded as a last resort in family placement. Although a growing number of lesbians and gay men are applying to adopt and foster and are successfully caring for children and youth, they remain an underused resource. With a national shortfall of adoptive and foster placements, and a national recruitment strategy to recruit and retain foster and adoptive persons, agencies need to ensure that they do not prejudice lesbian and gay applicants from coming forward as potential foster or adoptive resources for children and youth in need. In the chapters that follow, this book will:

- explore the stereotypes, myths, and prejudices that influence attitudes toward lesbians and gay men as parents;
- provide an overview of relevant research about lesbians and gay men as parents;
- examine how the development of policy and legislation over the years has influenced perceptions of lesbians and gay men as parents;
- explore approaches to developing strategies for recruitment of lesbians and gay men as adopters and foster parents;
- consider issues of best practice at all stages of the assessment process, including training issues and home studies that are lesbian and gay competent;

- explore ways for social workers to more effectively support lesbian and gay adopters and foster parents once they have been matched with a child or youth; and

- signpost further statewide and national resources and identify references, videos, and Web-based products that will provide further and ongoing information for social work staff.

Gay and Lesbian Fostering and Adoption

More than seven years ago, British social workers Stephen Hicks and Janet McDermott reminded us that "Lesbians and gay men have always been involved in having and raising children" (1999, p. 147). This was one of the first books to focus on the experiences of lesbian and gay parents in the United Kingdom, telling their stories firsthand and highlighting the issues that face adoption and fostering agencies in positively responding to gay people as potential parents and valuing them as a resource.

Lesbians and gay men in the United States have created families through adoption, foster care, and the establishment of kinship networks in a variety of ways (Weston, 1991). In some cases, lesbians and gay men became parents without disclosure or discussion of their sexuality with adoption and fostering agencies. As many lesbians and gay men have become able to live their lives more openly, however, more are considering parenthood in ways they might not have thought possible in the past.

For many lesbians and gay men, as pointed out by Hicks and McDermott (1999, p. 148), fostering and adoption is often not a second choice, as it may be for heterosexual men and women who are infertile (Turnner, 1999), but rather a first choice. Lesbians and gay men represent an untapped resource of potential parents for some of the many children who need substitute families. Although lesbian and gay men may have been historically discouraged from fostering or adoption, changes in legislation and policy over the past 10 years in some states reflect a more open attitude toward them as parents (Cooper & Cates, 2006; Pace, 2006).

The narratives Hicks and McDermott (1999) collected document experiences with social workers well, both positive and negative. The findings from this qualitative work suggest that the social work response to lesbian and gay applicants is varied and unpredictable. Although not all social workers are homophobic, a major issue seems to be the lack of policies to guide their practice. Going out on a limb to approve or work with a lesbian or gay parent or quietly implementing a borrowed idea from the U.S. military policy of "don't ask, don't tell" seemed to be common themes in these narratives and in the narratives gathered for the writing of this book. Inconsistencies between or within agencies and within states often existed in the ways that they responded to lesbian or gay applicants.

It is important that agencies and social workers are prepared for issues that will arise, both professionally and individually, in working with lesbian or gay prospective parents. Professionals need to be aware of inaccurate assumptions and stereotypes that have previously shaped policy and legislation and have informed practice. Social workers need to examine their own personal attitudes about lesbians and gay men. They need to be careful not to assume automatic parenting skills in heterosexual applicants, just as they need to be careful not to assume unsuitability for parenting in lesbian or gay applicants. The sexual orientation of a potential parent does not, of itself, indicate anything about his or her ability to care for children who may have had difficult experiences. Social workers need to explore openly with each individual or couple their experience and skills in relation to caring for a child or adolescent.

Researchers have identified two broad issues as having a negative effect on the assessment process for lesbians and gay men (Hicks & McDermott, 1999):

1. a lack of reliable information about the lives of lesbians and gay men, and

2. being defined by one's sexuality as a sole aspect of identity.

Acknowledging that specific issues arise for lesbian and gay applicants and dealing with them appropriately is an important part of assessment and ongoing support.

What *Is* a Family?

Many people, including some social work professionals, are uncomfortable discussing the idea of gay men and lesbians fostering or adopting children—the issue continues to evoke controversy and strong feelings.

Contemporary public debates about what constitutes a "proper" family can be put in context by considering some of the historical precedents and preconditions to these ideas. Ann Hartman and Joan Laird explored these themes in their book *Family-Centered Social Work Practice* (1983). In their text, the authors observed that family is vital to the historical formulation of nation and continues to act as a powerful metaphor and cultural institution for fixing ideas about identity today. Family has come to stand for moral order in the public sphere, which is one of the reasons why it is fought over with both such ferocity and such bitterness in the context of political rhetoric, the news media, and public welfare policies.

According to Hartman and Laird (1983), it is misleading to suggest that the traditional nuclear family no longer exists. It has, note the authors, existed as a transitional phase of some people's lives. Western nations are currently experiencing a variety of living arrangements, including some complex households that have not, as yet, been given a satisfactory label. Hartman and Laird (1983) offered the following broad definition of family, which may be useful for practitioners as a guide: "A family is a family when two or more persons decide to call themselves a family" (p. 24). The modern nuclear family, however, does exist, and it flourishes as an ideal: as a symbol, discourse, and powerful myth within the collective imagination.

Family structures in the United States have become increasingly varied. Millions of children are currently being raised by single or divorced parents, guardians, parents of different religions or races, gay or lesbian parents, and adoptive parents.

What do American families look like today? The following data provide readers with a snapshot of America's diverse families.

Overall

- Of the 102.5 million households in the United States, 69% are family households. The share of family households fell 10 percentage points between 1970 and 1990 (from 81% to 71%) but has dropped only 2 percentage points since (U.S. Census Bureau of Household and Family Statistics, 2004).
- The average U.S. family household consists of 3.18 people, down from 3.58 in 1970, but unchanged from 1990. Hispanic families are larger, with an average of 3.92 members, than either African American or non-Hispanic white families, which average 3.42 and 3.02 members, respectively (U.S. Census Bureau, 2004).

Single Parents

- Single parents account for 27% of family households with children younger than 18 *(U.S. Census Bureau, 2004)*.
- The number of single mothers (9.8 million) has remained constant over the past three years, and the number of single fathers has grown 25%, from 1.7 million in 1995 to 2.1 million in 1998, according to tabulations released by the U.S. Census Bureau (2004). Men now comprise one-sixth of the nation's 11.9-million single parents (U.S. Census Bureau, 2004).
- One in two children will live in a single-parent family at some point in childhood (Children's Defense Fund, 2004).

- One in three children is born to unmarried parents (Children's Defense Fund, 2004).
- The number of single mothers increased from 3 million to 10 million between 1970 and 2000 (U.S. Census Bureau, 2004).

Divorced Parents

- Nearly half of all marriages end in divorce (U.S. Census Bureau, 2004).
- More than one million children have parents who separate or divorce each year (National Commission on Children, 2005).
- More than half of Americans today have been, are, or will be in one or more stepfamily situations (Stepfamily Association of America, 2005).

Same-Gender Parents

- U.S. census data reveal that among heads of households who reported cohabitating with a same-gendered parent, 33% of women and 22% of men had a son or daughter younger than 18 years old living with them (Pace, 2006).
- The previous percentages correspond to about 65,000 gay fathers and 96,000 lesbian mothers who are heads of households and have at least one child living with them, and who are cohabitating with a partner (Pace, 2006).

Guardians and Foster Care

- Fiscal Year 2005 estimates as of September 30, 2005 were that 513,000 are in U.S. foster care (U.S. Department of Health and Human Services, [HHS], 2006)
- One child out of 25 lives with neither parent (Children's Defense Fund, 2004).
- The number of children in foster care who are being cared for by members of their extended family—grandparents, aunts, uncles—continues to increase. In 2004, kinship providers cared for about a third of the foster children (HHS, 2006).
- The 2000 U.S. census found that 2.4 million grandparents are the primary caregivers for the children in their families (U.S. Census Bureau, 2004).

Adoption

- In FY 2005, 114,000 children and youth were waiting to be adopted; of that group, 14,752 children were living in preadoptive homes; 63,235 were living in nonrelative foster homes, waiting for adoptions to be completed; and 21,147 were living in relative foster care. During this same time period, agencies finalized adoptions for more than 52,000 foster children (HHS, 2006).

- In FY 2005, 51,000 children and youth were adopted from the public foster care system (HHS, 2006).

- Of those adopted from the public foster care system, 62% were adopted by foster parents and by 25% by relatives, 15% by non-relatives (HHS, 2006).

- Of families adopting children from the public foster care system, 68% were married couples, 27% were headed by single females, 3% were headed by single males, and 2% were unmarried couples (HHS, 2006).

- According to national estimates, one million children in the United States live with adoptive parents, and 2% to 4% of American families include an adopted child (National Adoption Information Clearinghouse [NAIC], 2004).

- In 2000 and 2001, approximately 127,000 children were adopted annually in the United States (NAIC, 2004).

- Intercountry adoptions increased from 5% to 15% of total adoptions in the United States between 1992 and 2001 (NAIC, 2004).

- In 1996, more than 5.2 million children lived with one birthparent and either a stepparent or adoptive parent, up from 4.5 million in 1991 (U.S. Census Bureau, 2004).

Mixed-Race Families

- Interracial families are an ever-growing part of our national landscape. The 2000 census showed that 2.8 million children younger than 18 and nearly 7 million Americans of all ages identify as more than one race (U.S. Census Bureau, 2004).

- There are more than 4.5 million married and unmarried couples in the United States who are mixed racially or ethnically (U.S. Census Bureau, 2004).

Gay- and Lesbian-Headed and Unmarried-Partner Households

- Between 6 million and 10 million children of lesbian, gay, and bisexual parents currently live in the United States (Mallon, 2004).

- The number of unmarried partner households has increased by 72% in the last decade from 3 million in 1990 to more than 5 million in 2000. These figures include both same-sex and different-sex couples (U.S. Census Bureau, 2004).

- One-third of lesbian households and one-fifth of gay male households have children (U.S. Census Bureau, 2004).

- During the past decade, the number of same-sex households "grew significantly" in 10 states for which figures have been released: more than 700% in Delaware and Nevada; more than 400% in Vermont, Indiana, Louisiana, and Nebraska; and more than 200% in Connecticut, Illinois, Massachusetts, and Montana (U.S. Census Bureau, 2004).

Support for Adoption and Foster Parenting by Gay Men

The placement of children for adoption and family foster care has, as its main objective, the best interests of the child. Thus, the needs of each child or youth should be the primary determinant used in placing a child or youth in a family's home (especially because more than 50% of the 114,000 children freed for adoption are older than 9 years old). Issues of the foster or adoptive parent's sexual orientation may be important to consider in this decisionmaking process, but sexual orientation itself is not listed as an exclusionary criterion in the Child Welfare League of America's (CWLA's) adoption standards (2000) or in the CWLA *Standards of Excellence for Family Foster Care Services* (1995, pp. 5–8). Section 5.8 of the adoption standards states:

> Sexual preferences should not be the sole criteria on which the suitability of adoptive parents is based. Consideration should be given to other personality and maturity factors and the ability of the applicant to meet the specific needs of the individual child.

In March of 2000, the North American Council on Adoptable Children adopted a policy statement on gay and lesbian foster and adoptive parenting that reaffirmed CWLA's statement, stating: "Everyone with the potential to successfully parent a child in foster care or adoption is entitled to fair and equal consideration regardless of sexual orientation" (p. 26).

Becoming a Lesbian or Gay Parent: Making Decisions

Lesbians and gay men become foster or adoptive parents for some of the same reasons that heterosexual people adopt or foster children (Mallon, 1998b, 2004; Pies, 1990). Some pursue adoption or foster care as a single person; some seek to create a family as a same-gender couple. Although many common themes of adoption and foster care exist (Brodzinsky & Schechter, 1990; Lancaster, 1996; Melina, 1998), which readers will see reflected in the pages that follow, they also have some unique features. Unlike their heterosexual counterparts, who couple, get pregnant, and give birth, gay and lesbian individuals and couples who wish to parent must consider many other variables in deciding whether to become parents. First, the couple must decide how they should go about creating a family: adoption (Mallon, 2004), foster parenting (Ricketts, 1991; Ricketts & Achtenberg, 1990), surrogacy (Bernfeld, 1995; Menichiello, 2006), or alternative insemination (Agigian, 2004).

Second, the couple must decide whether to be open about their sexual orientation. Although it is legal for lesbians and gay men to adopt, some couples fear that they would not be able to adopt if they disclosed their orientation. Some lesbians and gay men do choose to be open about their sexual orientation, whereas others identify their partner as "a friend" who will help raise the child. Because in most states only one parent can be recognized as the legal parent, this establishes, as Hartman (1996) pointed out, "an asymmetrical relationship between the two parents and the child" (p. 81). This asymmetry occurs on multiple levels: from school visits, to medical permission forms, to eligibility for Social Security survivors' benefits in the case of the death of a co-parent, to lack of support from family members, to requirements for support and visiting arrangements in the case of a separation.

Lesbian and gay individuals who choose to adopt as single parents will also face stresses that may be more unique to single parenting than to their gay identification (Feigelman & Silverman, 1983; Marindin, 1997; Melina, 1998, p. 292). But it is not all struggle and hardship—on the positive side, gay men and lesbians who choose to create families have the advantage of redefining and reinventing their own meaning for family and parenting, precisely because they exist outside of the traditionally defined family. They have the unique opportunity to break out of preconceived gender roles and be a new kind of parent to a child (Benkov, 1994).

Trends in Adoption: Dilemmas Agencies Face in Accepting Gay and Lesbian Prospective Parents

Numerous child welfare agencies across the country have broken through their own organizational bias against lesbians and gay men and are already placing children with same-sex parents (Evan B. Donaldson, 2003). The Evan B. Donaldson Adoption Institute issued a report in October 2003 that found that 60% of the country's adoption agencies accept applications from same-sex couples. The study further showed that 40% of U.S. agencies have already placed children in homes with gay or lesbian parents. In a report analyzing 2000 census data, Arc's Family Net project and the Urban Institute also found that same-sex parents are 1.7% more likely to have adopted than all other households.

But by and large, few child welfare agencies seem to be openly discussing this process. Agency heads might be concerned that it will attract negative attention to their agency or somehow be divisive among staff. A large adoption and foster parenting network exists within gay communities across the country, as well as a virtual community found on many Internet websites, all of which assist gay men and lesbians interested in adoption or foster parenting in identifying the names and address of "safe" child welfare agencies where they can be certified (see http://www.aclu.org/lgbt/parenting/index.html, www.aclu.org/lgbt/youth/index.html, and www.lambdalegal.org).

Moving Toward a Policy of Inclusiveness

Although President Clinton's signing of the historic Adoption and Safe Families Act of 1997 (ASFA, P.L. 105-89; Baker, 1997) does not directly address the issue of lesbian and gay adoption per se, this legislation signaled the culmination of more than two decades of work to make it easier to move tens of thousands of children out of foster care and into permanent families, including families headed by lesbians and gay men. ASFA provides unprecedented financial incentives to states to increase adoption and helps child welfare providers speed children out of foster care and into permanent families by setting meaningful time limits for child welfare decisions, by clarifying which family situations call for reasonable reunification efforts and which do not, and by making the safety of children the paramount concern in placement decisions (CWLA, 1998). The evidence documenting the damage to children caused by multiple foster care placements is unambiguous (Fanshel, 1982; Fanshel & Shinn, 1978; Festinger, 1983; Maas & Engler, 1959). Minimizing foster care drift and emphasizing permanency planning for children (Mallon & Leashore, 2002; Maluccio, Fein, & Olmstead, 1986; Pelton, 1991; Pierce, 1992) have been primary focuses of child and family services for more than two decades, and they were reaffirmed in President Clinton's signing of AFSA.

Historically perceived as a preferential service granted only to those couples who were white and infertile, and who could afford to take a healthy, same-race infant into their home, adoption is now viewed in a much broader context. Contemporary adoption has made it possible for a broader range of children to be adopted—children of color, children with a range of disabilities, children with medical and developmental issues, and preschoolers and adolescents.

Similarly, policies have made it possible for a broader range of adults to adopt, including foster parents, families of color, single individuals (both male and female), older individuals, individuals with disabilities, and families across a broad economic range. At one time or another, many of these groups were excluded from the adoption process. Inclusion of some of these groups caused great controversy when initiated. In the process of moving toward inclusiveness, however, many professionals voiced concern about lowering the standard of adoption and thereby damaging the field.

The trend toward inclusiveness, and a broader understanding of who makes a suitable parent, has had a major effect on the more than 513,000 children in out-of-home care, some of whom have waited for extended periods for permanent homes. Such changes have allowed children and youth previously considered unadoptable, or not suitable for family foster care, to be provided with permanent homes with caring adults, some of whom are gay and lesbian. Although accurate statistics on the number of gay and lesbian people do not exist, it has been estimated that up to 10% of the population (25 million individuals) identify as having a sexual orientation as other than heterosexual. Excluding 25 million individuals from becoming adoptive parents solely on the basis of sexual orientation seems preposterous considering how many children and youth are in need of permanent families.

Although some child welfare agencies are struggling to develop policies about gay and lesbian parenting, many agencies appear to believe "the less said the better" (Sullivan, 1995, p. 3) and therefore do not publicize the fact that they place children with gay and lesbian people. Perhaps they are afraid of being stigmatized as "the gay adoption or foster care agency." Organizational structures, which operate in the absence of written policies, frequently compel staff members to develop their own policies. The lack of written policies, in and of itself, is a strategy that many child welfare agency executives and boards have permitted to exist with respect to the issue of gay and lesbian adoption and foster parenting. When individuals design their own policies to guide agency practice, the agencies run the risk of personal, cultural, and religious bias. Child welfare agencies, some of which continue to avoid written policies, do not provide the opportunity for the community to resolve the issue. Policies responding to the needs of children and families need to be written and clearly communicated to all interested groups.

Conclusion

I would not argue that all gay and lesbian people should be adoptive or foster parents. In the same way, I would never argue that all non-gay people would make suitable adoptive parents. In the pages that follow, the stories of some adoptive and foster parents are evidence that many lesbians and gay men are appropriate and loving parents to their children. Thousands of untold narratives exist by other lesbian and gay adoptive and foster parents, who are caring parents for children and youth who needed temporary or permanent families. The question is not whether gay men or lesbians will be approved as adoptive or foster parents, but how publicly they will be, and whether these families will be offered the same fair process and open opportunity as non-gay people who seek to adopt or foster. Sidestepping the issue of adoption and foster parenting by lesbians and gay men, or pretending that the issue doesn't exist, does not protect children. It runs counter to the ASFA legislation and prevents some children and youth from being part of a loving family, which all children deserve.

Child welfare agencies are responsible for ensuring a timely and appropriate adoptive family for every child who needs one. In meeting this responsibility, child welfare agencies must explore all potential resources for all children and youth awaiting placement in a family, including qualified lesbians and gay men who wish to parent and are eager to open their hearts and lives to children and youth in need.

Lesbian and gay fostering and adoption may challenge the traditional notions of family and in turn may challenge practitioners to examine their own views of what constitutes a family.

The chapters that follow review foundation-level knowledge that is required for social workers who will work with this population, discuss the research about lesbian and gay parenting, highlight the relevant legislation and policy initiatives from a legal context on a national level, illuminate recruitment strategies for tapping into this under-used resource pool, and finally, provide some practical guidance for those conducting assessments and providing support for lesbian and gay foster and adoptive families. In meeting the needs of the children and youth who are waiting for placements, agencies must explore all potential resources for these children, including lesbians and gay men who wish to parent.

CHAPTER 2

LESBIAN AND GAY IDENTITY

THIS CHAPTER WILL EXAMINE:

- the image and demography of the lesbian and gay population,
- terminology,
- common questions and presumptions about gay men and lesbians, and
- coming out and lesbian and gay identity.

The Image and Demography of the Lesbian and Gay Population

It is inaccurate to talk about a lesbian and gay community as if it is uniform or easily identifiable. As with all communities, the lesbian and gay community is diverse in terms of how individuals wish to define themselves and live their lives.

The images that the popular media most perpetuates about gay men and lesbians are the stereotypes of the effeminate, white, meticulously groomed and dressed, middle- to upper-socioeconomic-class, urban man living in a fabulously decorated house or apartment, or the butch, short-haired, jewelry- and make-up-free, motorcycle-riding woman who carries her wallet in her back pocket. Being gay or lesbian has also perhaps been viewed in some quarters as being only a "white thing."

But the reality is that although some may fit those stereotypes, gay men and lesbians are as diverse as any other subgroup of the general population, and they are part of every race, culture, ethnic group, religious group, socioeconomic affiliation, and family in the United States today.

Lesbians and gay men are frequently socialized to hide their sexual orientation, and therefore, most form part of an invisible population. A search of the 2000 U.S. census data yielded no results using the terms *lesbian, gay,* or *homosexual,* so it is not possible to accurately document the size of the gay and lesbian population. It is estimated, however, that about 10% of the U.S. population identify as lesbian or gay. In addition, in many areas of the United States (mostly outside of urban areas), it is still relatively unsafe for most lesbian or gay people to live openly and acknowledge their sexual orientation.

Terminology

Language is often a source of confusion and misinformation, and as such, it is important that service providers have accurate definitions. Heterosexual oriented care practitioners are often unfamiliar or uncomfortable with the vernacular of the gay and lesbian "culture." It should be recognized that as with any subculture—particularly that of oppressed groups—language is constantly changing. Usage may vary with different generations, geographic areas of the country, socioeconomic status, or cultural backgrounds. Which terms are acceptable and which are offensive varies widely and is also culturally dependent.

The use of the word *homosexual* in describing individuals and same-sex relationships may also be inaccurate. When referring to people, as opposed to behavior, *homosexual* is considered derogatory and places the emphasis on sex. The preferred terms used by most are *gay* and *lesbian,* which stress cultural and social matters more than sex. In addition, prior to 1972, the term *homosexual* was a diagnostic term used to pathologize gay men and lesbians.

So that adoption and foster care social workers are clear about terminology and language, the following describes terms that relate to lesbians and gay men, and to sex, gender, and sexuality.

Sex, Gender, and Sexuality

The English noun *gender* is derived from the Old French word *genre*, meaning "kind of thing." It goes back to the Latin word *genus* (meaning "kind" or "species"). *Gender* is often, but decreasingly, used as a synonym for *sex*, which refers to the physical anatomical differences that are commonly used to differentiate male from female.

Many people, among them social scientists, use *sex* to refer to the biological division into male and female, and *gender* to refer to gender roles assigned to people on the basis of their apparent sex and other associated factors. Society tends to assign some social roles to males and others to females (as society perceives their sex).

A person's gender is usually assigned at birth. The "male" or "female" recorded on the birth certificate can affect much of what happens to that child, socially, for the rest of his or her life. Gender is social, cultural, psychological, and historical. It is used to describe people and their roles in society, the way they dress, and how they are meant to behave.

It is assumed by some that sex, gender, and sexuality naturally follow on from each other, but different societies and cultures have had very different notions of sex, gender, and sexuality and how people express them. It is perhaps more helpful to consider "What is sexuality, and how do people in different places and at different times understand their bodies and desires?" *Sexuality* is usually defined as the expression of sexual desire.

Sexual Orientation

This is the commonly accepted term for the direction of a person's sexual attraction, emotional or physical attraction, and its expression. Examples of sexual orientation are heterosexuality, homosexuality, and bisexuality. In a sense, sexual orientation is a social construct, and a relatively new one, most likely determined by a combination of continually interacting sociocultural influences and biological tendencies. Most cultures have a sexual object preference for the opposite sex.

For many years, the common assumption, shared by many scientists and religious communities, was that the natural and normal human sexual orientation is exclusively for the opposite sex (i.e., heterosexual). In 1976, the historian Michel Foucault argued that homosexuality as a concept did not exist as such in the 18th century, that people instead spoke of sodomy (which involved specific sexual acts, regardless of the sex or sexuality of the people involved). Sexual studies carried out during and after the 1950s led psychologists and doctors to recognize homosexuality as a second exclusive orientation. Since then, similar acceptance has grown for nonexclusive orientations, such as bisexuality.

Heterosexuality

This term relates to sexual attraction, both physical and emotional, which is primarily directed toward people of the opposite gender.

Homosexuality

This term relates to sexual attraction, both physical and emotional, which is primarily directed toward people of the same gender. The word *homosexual* translates literally as "of the same sex," being a hybrid of the Greek prefix *homo-* meaning "same" (as distinguished from the Latin root *homo* meaning *human*) and the Latin root *sex* meaning "sex."

Although some early writers used the adjective *homosexual* to refer to any single-gender context (such as the Roman Catholic clergy or an all-girls' school), today the term implies a sexual aspect. The term *homosocial* is now used to describe single-sex contexts that are not specifically sexual. Older terms for homosexuality, such as *homophilia* and *inversion* (in which a gay individual would be called a "homophile" or an "invert") have fallen into disuse. The term *homosexual* can be used as a noun or adjective to describe same-sex-oriented individuals as well as their sexual attractions and behaviors.

It is recommend that the terms *homosexual* and *homosexuality* be avoided—in particular, describing individuals as homosexual may be offensive, partially because of the negative clinical association of the word, stemming from its use in describing same-sex attraction as a pathological state, before homosexuality was removed from lists of mental disorders. For example, the American Psychiatric Association's 1968 list of mental disorders still regarded homosexuality as confused or disturbed sexuality. In the United States in 1975, the *Journal of the American Medical Association* was still publishing articles on possible treatments for ego-dystonic homosexuality,* including hormonal therapy and aversion therapy. It was not until the late 1980s that journals began to focus on research and articles that were lesbian and gay affirming in their approach to treatment.

Bisexuality

This term refers to sexual attraction toward people of both genders. Someone who identifies as bisexual is attracted to and may form sexual and affectionate relationships with both men and women, though not necessarily at the same time. The term may refer to a sociopolitical identity or to sexual behavior, or both. Most known societies have included people who have exhibited some degree of bisexuality.

Although bisexuality is an identified sexual orientation, it is sometimes transitional for those coming to terms with their lesbian or gay identity. Some people identify as bisexual before identifying as gay or lesbian, because bisexuality can represent a mediating position between homosexual and heterosexual in the traditional cultural system.

---

* Ego-dystonic homosexuality is a psychosexual disorder in which an individual has persistent distress associated with same-gender sexual orientation and is unable to initiate or maintain heterosexual relationships, usually experiencing a strong need to change the behavior or, at least, to alleviate the distress associated with the gay or lesbian sexual orientation.

Gay

In addition to meaning "merry," "joyous," or "glad," *gay* also means homosexual. *Gay* also refers to homosexually oriented ideas (e.g., literature or values). The word *gay* has had a sexual meaning since at least the 19th century (and possibly earlier; Chauncey, 1994). In Victorian England, female and male prostitutes were called "gay" because they dressed gaily. Eventually, "gay boys" (male prostitutes) became used as a term for any male homosexual. It has also been claimed that *gay* was an acronym for "Good as You," another popular etymology with its supposed origin emanating from a street called Gay Street, in New York's West Village, a focal point of lesbian and gay culture. The term also seems, from documentary evidence, to have existed in New York as a code word in the 1940s, where the question, "Are you gay?" would denote more than it might have seemed to outsiders (Chauncey, 1994).

Gay can be used to refer only to male homosexuals. Used inclusively, it refers to homosexual men and women, and arguably to bisexuals. When used in the phrase *the gay community*, it may also include transgender people and transsexuals, although this is also a subject of some debate, and these issues will not be fully addressed in this book.

Gay originally was used purely as an adjective ("He is a gay man" or "He is gay"). *Gay* is now also used as a collective noun (e.g., "Gays are opposed to that policy"), but rarely as a singular noun ("He is a gay"). When used as an adjective not describing a person who is part of the gay community (as many children and youth are now popularizing in school settings, e.g., "That shirt is so gay"), the term *gay* is purely pejorative and deeply offensive. The derogatory implication is that the object (or person) in question is inferior, weak, effeminate, or just stupid.

Lesbian

A lesbian is a woman whose homosexual orientation is self-defined, affirmed, or acknowledged as such. *Lesbian* also refers to female homosexually oriented (and can refer to women-oriented) ideas, communities, or varieties of cultural expression.

The word *lesbian* originally referred to an inhabitant of the Greek island of Lesbos. It came to have its current meaning because of the ancient Greek poet Sappho, who lived on Lesbos; some of her poems concerned love between women. Whether Sappho was a lesbian, in the modern meaning of the term, or simply a poet who described lesbians, is open to question. Nevertheless, this association with Sappho led to the term *sapphism* being used as another term for lesbianism.

Transgendered

Transgender, is a term created by people with trans-histories to refer to trans-people and is now generally considered an umbrella term encompassing many different identites. It is commonly used to describe and individual who is seen as "gender-different." Outside the transgender communities, people identified as transgender are usually perceived through a dichotomous lens and are commonly described as transgressing gender norms, gender variant or gender deviant. This traditional mis-reading predicates a conception of transgender within a pathologically oriented perspecive framed in a language layered in heterosexist, sesist, bigenderist, and transphobic context and meaning.

Transgender is often used as a euphemistic synonym for transsexual people. One set of reasoning for this is that it removes the conceptual image of "sex" in *transsexual* that implies transsexuality is sexually motivated, which it is not. *Transgender* is also used to describe behavior or feelings that cannot be catego-rized into other defined categories, for example, people living in a gender role that is different from the one they were assigned at birth, but who do not wish to undergo any or all of the available medical options, or people who do not wish to identify themselves as transsexuals, either men or women, and consider that they fall between genders or transcend gender.

Transvestite/Cross-Dresser

This is a person who, for any reason, wears the clothing of a gender other than that to which they were assigned at birth. Cross-dressers may have no desire or intention of adopting the behaviors or practices common to that other gender and do not nec-essarily wish to undergo medical procedures to facilitate physical changes. Contrary to common belief, most male-bodied cross-dressers prefer female partners.

Bull Dyke, Fag, and Queer

These terms are sometimes used to refer negatively to lesbians and gay men. They are equivalent to hate terms and epithets used against racial and ethnic minorities. A political usage exists for words such as *queer, dyke,* or *faggot* by some gays and lesbians who, in a reclamation process, redefine and use with pride words formerly used as pejorative. Because these words still carry a negative connotation in society, however, their positive usage is restricted to political lesbians and gay men active in the recla-mation struggle and as words used by in-group members to define themselves.

Drag

The term *drag queen* originates in Polari, the language of gay men in England in the early part of the last century. *Drag* meant *clothes*, and was also theatre slang for a woman's costume worn by a male actor. A *queen* is an effeminate gay man. Drag is a part of Western gay culture—drag involves wearing highly exaggerated and outrageous costumes or imitating movie and music stars of the opposite sex. It is a form of performing art practiced by drag queens and kings. Female-bodied people who perform in usually exaggerated men's clothes and personae are called drag kings, though this term has a wider meaning than *drag queen.*

Drag kings should not just be seen as female equivalents of drag queens, because the term covers a much wider field of gender performance and political activism. Gender identity among drag kings is far more varied, too. Drag kings are largely a phenomenon of lesbian culture; they have only recently begun to gain the fame or focus that drag queens have known for years.

Heterosexism (or Heterocentrism or Heterosexualism)

This is the assumption that everyone or a particular person is heterosexual. It does not necessarily imply hostility toward other sexual orientations (as does homophobia), but is merely a failure to recognize their existence. Heterocentrism is culturally, religiously, and socially sanctioned by most major institutions in American culture, including the family.

Homophobia

This term is most frequently used to describe any sort of opposition to homosexual behavior or the political causes associated with homosexuality, though this opposition may more accurately be called "anti-gay bias."

The term also describes a phobia triggered by an encounter (in oneself or others) with same-sex physical attraction, love, and sexuality. The term was originally described by George Weinberg (1973), the clinical psychologist who coined the term, to mean a morbid and irrational fear of homosexuals.

Homo-ignorant

Homo-ignorant is a term developed to describe individuals with a very limited knowledge about gays, lesbians, bisexuals, and transgender individuals.

Coming Out

Coming out, a distinctively lesbian and gay phenomenon (see Cass, 1979, 1984; Coleman, 1981; Troiden, 1979, 1989), is defined as "the developmental process through which gay and lesbian people recognise their sexual orientation and integrate this knowledge into their personal and social lives" (De Monteflores & Schultz, 1978, p. 59). Coming out is the process of first recognizing and then acknowledging nonheterosexual orientation in oneself, and then disclosing it to others. Coming out often occurs in stages and is a nonlinear process. Coming out can also be used to mean "disclosure," as in "I just came out to my parents."

Disclosure

The point at which a lesbian or gay man discloses his or her sexual orientation to another person. It is not appropriate to use terms such as *discovered, admitted, revealed, found out,* or *declared,* which are pejorative terms, suggesting judgment.

Being Out

This term is used to describe a person who is open about their sexual orientation to friends, family, colleagues, and society. Not everyone who is "out" is out to all of these groups; some people may be out to their family, but not to their colleagues.

Being Closeted or in the Closet

These terms refer to someone who is not open about his or her sexual orientation. This person, for his or her own personal reasons, chooses to hide his or her sexuality from others.

Common Questions and Presumptions

This section deals with some of the myths and questions that social workers may have about lesbians and gay men. In the absence of accurate information, many professionals rely on their own knowledge, which may be shaped by stereotypes and myths. We are brought up in a society that presumes heterosexuality as the norm, and this is expressed through language and behavior, which in turn are often based on myths and stereotypes. The following are some common questions and presumptions.

How do you know if you are lesbian or gay?
For the most part, knowing whether you are gay or lesbian is all about paying attention to feelings of attraction. It is very difficult for many people to be hon-

est with themselves about same-gender attraction because society is, in general, unaccepting of lesbians and gay men. Some young people know they are gay or lesbian early in life—as early as 10 years old. Others do not have or acknowledge these feelings until much later. Coming out is a process that can occur at any time in the life cycle, not just during childhood or adolescence.

Can someone be lesbian or gay without ever having had a gay or lesbian experience or relationship?

Yes. Some lesbians and gay men have never had a sexual relationship with another person, yet know they are lesbian or gay. Sexual orientation has more to do with internal feelings—one's sense of "affectional fit," rather than actual sexual experience.

Can someone have gay or lesbian feelings and not be lesbian or gay? Can someone have heterosexual feelings and not be a heterosexual?

Yes. Human sexuality is very complex and not easily separated into rigid categories. It is perfectly natural for a gay man or lesbian to have feelings of attraction for someone of the opposite gender, just as it is perfectly natural for a heterosexual person to have feelings of attraction for a person of the same gender. Although almost everyone experiences these feelings at one time or another, they can be confusing. Many people struggling with issues of sexual orientation will test out their feelings with both males and females. It is important to remember that people will eventually "be who they are." Nothing that anyone tells them or says to encourage them or dissuade them will change their sexual orientation. Sexuality and sexual or gender identity is a very complex area of practice, and social workers must develop skills for dealing with the ambiguity of sexual identity.

If you have had a same-gender sexual experience, does that make you gay or lesbian?

Being lesbian or gay is not just about sexual behavior. The sexual aspect of a lesbian or gay person's life is, of course, important, but to focus exclusively on those aspects is a mistake. Knowing that you are lesbian or gay is more than just sexual behavior. Social workers need to be clear for themselves and for the clients with whom they work that sexual orientation and sexuality involve many aspects of identity and relationship that go beyond sexual behavior.

How many lesbians and gay men are there?

Although a great deal of discussion about the size of the lesbian and gay population has taken place, the reality is that because it is still stigmatizing for some people to identify as such, many lesbians and gay men hide their sexuality. It is therefore very difficult to ascertain how many lesbians and gay men there are. The most common estimate—that 10% of the population identify as lesbian or gay—is derived from research conducted by Kinsey, Pomeroy, and Martin (1948) and Kinsey, Pomeroy, Martin, and Gebhard (1953).

Have lesbians and gay men always existed?

Yes. Evidence abounds of the existence of homosexuality throughout history, as depicted in art, literature, and music. Famous lesbians and gay men throughout history include: Plato; Alexander the Great; Leonardo da Vinci; Michelangelo; James I; Tchaikovsky; Oscar Wilde; Sir Ian McKellen, award-winning British actor; Virginia Woolf; Noel Coward; Cole Porter; Niki Giovanni, poet; Billy Strayhorn, songwriter; Pedro Almodóvar, Spanish filmmaker; Michelle Cliff, Jamaican writer; Christopher Isherwood, British writer; Audre Lorde, poet and writer; Vita Sackville-West, British writer; Ellen DeGeneres, comedian; Barney Frank (D-MA), U.S. Representative; James Baldwin, writer; Langston Hughes; poet; Melissa Etheridge, singer; Reverend Peter Gomes, chaplain of Harvard University; Mary Cheney, daughter of U.S. vice-president Dick Cheney; and Martina Navratilova, tennis champion.

How do you become lesbian or gay?

You cannot become lesbian or gay, any more than a person becomes heterosexual. Because sexual identity emanates from one's internal sense of fit, most lesbians and gay men become aware of these feelings as they grow up. Exactly where these feelings come from and why remains an unknown factor.

Are some people born lesbian or gay?

Preliminary research evidence (LeVay, 1994; Loehlin & McFadden, 2003; Savic, Berglund, & Lindström, 2005; Wade, 2005) suggests that there is a genetic and biological basis for sexual orientation. Although many gay males, some bisexuals, some transgender people, and some lesbians recall that they have always known they were "different," others do not agree with the "gay from birth" philosophy. The research in this area is very limited.

Is being lesbian or gay a choice for some people?

Just as heterosexual people do not choose their sexual orientation, the large majority of lesbians and gay men do not choose theirs. The only real choice that most lesbian and gay people have to deal with is whether to be open about their orientation. Some lesbians and gay men, however, do envision their entire identity as a social construction—a series of choices that they make about their lives.

These individuals feel that it is their choice, not society's, to determine how to live and what to do.

Can someone be seduced into being lesbian or gay?

No, it is simply not possible for someone to be seduced into being gay, any more than a gay man or a lesbian could be seduced into being heterosexual.

Are lesbians or gay men more likely to abuse a child?

No. The most likely person to abuse a child, according to researchers (Jenny, Roesler, & Poyer, 1994) is a heterosexual male who is known to the child's family. Despite this clear evidence, however, the terms *gay* and *child sexual abuser* are very often seen as synonymous.

Does the experience of being sexually abused as a child make you lesbian or gay?

Although some lesbians and gay men were sexually abused as children, just as some heterosexual men and women were sexually abused, no evidence suggests that being sexually abused makes someone gay or lesbian.

Are lesbians and gay men the way they are because they have not met the right man or woman?

No. In fact, many gay men and lesbians have been married or had partners of the opposite gender. Being lesbian or gay is not a matter of meeting the right person of the opposite gender again; it is about finding the right internal sense of fit with a person, which usually is a person of the same gender.

Couldn't lesbians and gay men really be heterosexual if they tried?

Many lesbians and gay men have tried to be heterosexual. Being lesbian or gay is so condemned by some in society that many lesbian and gay people pretend to be heterosexual, at least for part of their lives. Some try for a lifetime, never acting on or acknowledging their true feelings. Some find ways to adapt to their feelings through furtive relationships, and others remain married for years.

How can you tell if a person is lesbian or gay?

Although at one time, many people thought that lesbians and gay men were identifiable through stereotypical mannerisms, affectations, dress, and so on, the only real way to tell if someone is lesbian or gay is if he or she tells you. Too often, social workers continue to look for the stereotypical nonconforming behaviors or mannerisms, but by and large, lesbians and gay men are a very diverse group that comes in all colors, cultures, religions, sizes, ages, temperaments, and degrees of masculinity and femininity.

Are lesbians and gay men normal?

If normal means the majority, then gay and lesbian persons are not normal by this definition. If you are left-handed, you are not in the majority, and yet people would view you as normal. Most lesbians and gay men believe that their sexual orientation is a normal variation on the continuum of sexual orientation.

Is there a lesbian or gay culture?

Lesbians and gay men exist in all races, cultures, ethnic backgrounds, religions, and social classes. Inasmuch as lesbians and gay men adopt the norms of their particular cultures, lesbians and gay men also have their own language, humor, styles of dress, social events, and norms. Lesbian and gay culture is diverse, so it is important for workers to listen carefully to the individuals they are working with and understand what being lesbian or gay means for their clients.

Is there a lesbian or gay lifestyle?

Most lesbian and gay people object to this term because it trivializes lesbians' and gay men's lives. If you are a lesbian or gay man, then you have a life, not a lifestyle. Just as no such thing as a heterosexual lifestyle exists, there is no such thing as a lesbian or gay lifestyle.

Do gay men hate women, and do lesbians hate men?

Obvious tensions exist between men and women. Some gay men hate women and some lesbians hate men, just like some heterosexual men hate women and some heterosexual women hate men. But, in general, gay men do not hate women and lesbians do not hate men.

Do gay men and lesbians hate heterosexual people?

Some lesbian and gay people have hostile feelings for heterosexuals, but generally, the answer to this question is no. Lesbians and gay men have experienced discrimination and prejudice at the hands of heterosexuals, yet many have heterosexuals among their friends.

Why do so many people have trouble accepting lesbians and gay men?

Discussion of sex and sexuality makes many people feel uncomfortable. Homosexuality in particular appears to generate strong feelings in some people. Many people have difficulty accepting lesbians and gay men because of their religious beliefs or moral perspective. Some people are uncomfortable dealing with lesbians and gay men because of their own biases. It is important to begin to understand the nature of homophobia that exists in society, and as part of this be willing to engage in examining our own attitudes and values in relation to sexualities that are different from our own.

Coming Out and Self-Identity

From a practice perspective, it is essential that adoption and foster care social workers acknowledge that coming out is a process that can occur at any stage of an individual's life. Gay men and lesbians may be out in some situations or to certain family members or associates, and not others—some may be out only to lesbian or gay friends, others to friends who are not lesbian and gay. Still others who self-identify as lesbian or gay are out to everyone—family, friends, employers, coworkers, and the larger community. Some people may never come out to anyone besides themselves. It is, in fact, possible for someone to stay in the closet even to themselves, although great psychological consequences must be paid for doing so.

Coming out is a very personal and unique situation for each individual; homophobia is still so prevalent in society that many lesbians and gay men choose to stay closeted for many different reasons. African American and disabled lesbians and gay men may live with the dual tensions associated with coming out and being in a minority and, as such, may opt to stay closeted to avoid further pressures.

Coming out as a lesbian or gay man during adolescence may be a very different experience than coming out as an adult. Consequently, some people move through the process smoothly, accepting their sexuality, making social contacts, and finding a good fit in their environments. Others are unnerved by their sexuality, vacillating in their conviction, hiding in their uneasiness, and struggling to find their place. In addition, there are different levels of "outness" or "openness" about one's sexual orientation.

Race and ethnicity can also affect the coming-out process. African American people, many of whom have experienced significant stress related to oppression and racism based on skin color or ethnicity, may experience even greater difficulty coming out, especially within the family context (Greene, 1994; Savin-Williams & Rodriguez, 1993; Walters, 1998). There have been many black lesbians and gay men throughout history; some of them are listed in this publication.

Individuals in the African American, Latino, and American Indian communities who identify themselves as lesbian or gay may become aware of their difference in adolescence, and they must not only deal with the stigma in their own cultural and racial community, but must also find a supportive lesbian or gay community to which they can relate. The lesbian and gay community is often a microcosm of society, and many African American gay men and lesbians confront racism there. To sustain oneself in three distinct communities requires an enormous effort and can also produce stress for both the adolescent and the adult (J. Hunter & Schaecher, 1987; Morales, 1989; Roscoe, 1987).

Internalized Homophobia

When I first came out, at 25, I was really turned off by effeminate gay men. Drag queens really made me crazy. I didn't want anyone thinking that I was like that. After a while, I realized how homophobic that kind of thinking was—I mean, what, did I think I was better than them because I was butch? In reality, whether I wanted people to see me as masculine or not, some people in society would always think of gay men as "fairies," and there wasn't anything I could do to change that. I guess it took me a while to get comfortable about my gay identity and to realize that as gay people, we are a very diverse group, which includes drag queens and butch men.

Some psychological research suggests that internalized homophobia is a normal part of the process of coming out (Forstein, 1988; Malyon, 1982; Shidlo, 1994). Lesbians and gay men people grow up in a heterosexual world that continually tells them they are wrong. They are taught to believe that heterosexuality is the only option and that a gay or lesbian identity is a perversion. Thus, many young lesbians and gay men fall victim to Shidlo's (1994) definition of internalized homophobia: "A set of negative attitudes and affects toward homosexuality in other persons and toward homosexual features in oneself" (p. 178). These feelings can significantly impede the self-acceptance process that many gay men and women must go through to come out.

Psychology researchers Fassinger and Miller (as cited in Mayfield, 2001) explained that two models of identity development for gay men and lesbians exist: (1) an individual development of sexual identity that includes acceptance of a lesbian or gay orientation, and (2) the development of a group membership identity, involving the acceptance of membership in an oppressed group and developing affiliations within that group (p. 55). Thus, an individual could accept himself or herself but not accept the lesbian or gay community in general. Negative attitudes toward lesbian and gay culture may be seen as an alternative type of internalized homophobia.

Internalized homophobia is rooted in the shame our society places on gay or lesbian identity. Overcoming that shame in oneself is the first step toward self-acceptance and, in turn, acceptance of the lesbian and gay community.

Conclusion

This chapter summarizes the images and demography of the lesbian and gay population in the United States. It defines commonly used terms and professional terminology for social workers who are working with or intend to work with lesbians and gay men. In addition, it has identified and dispelled myths and stereotypes about lesbians and gay men that workers frequently use in the absence of accurate information. It illuminates some common questions and presumptions about gay men and lesbians for the reader. Finally, it discusses and highlights the process of coming out and develops a discussion of lesbian and gay identity for the social work practitioner.

THE LEGAL CONTEXT

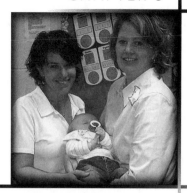

THE POLITICAL DEBATE THAT HAS TAKEN PLACE over the past four decades has highlighted the level of homophobia that permeates our society. It is worth noting there are now 17 states (California, Connecticut, Hawaii, Illinois, Maine, Maryland, Massachusetts, Minnesota, Nevada, New Hampshire, New Jersey, New Mexico, New York, Rhode Island, Vermont, Washington, and Wisconsin) and the District of Columbia with antidiscrimination laws in the United States. All of these laws protect at least lesbian and gay employees; some go further. In addition, municipalities across the country are also adopting civil rights ordinances to cover lesbians and gay men in areas such as employment, public accommodations, housing, credit, union practices, and education (Human Rights Campaign, 2005).

Legislation and policy over the past 50 years have reflected discrimination against gay men and lesbians in the United States. This chapter provides an overview of the changes in U.S. law and policy relating to lesbians and gay men in two particular areas of life:

- their sexual practices, and
- their freedom and right to be parents.

Positive changes have occurred in the last 10 years in terms of a political shift in attitudes, which are reflected in legislation; however, the day-to-day realities of life for many lesbians and gay men have not been affected by these shifts—particularly in the areas of family life and parenting. Legislation and policy have been shaped by, and in turn have influenced, attitudes toward gay and lesbian relationships and parenting, and they have also influenced decisionmaking in terms of what is in the best interests of children in terms of family life.

Acutely conflicting attitudes toward a lesbian or gay sexual orientation share an uneasy existence in Western society (See also Cooper & Cates, 2006, Chapter 2 for a review of legal issues). The range of perspectives is reflected in legislation, legal decisionmaking, social policy design, and academic scholarship. The range of attitudes ranging from disapproval, to pity, to insouciance, to respect appears in both the legal and social welfare communities and is firmly rooted in heterocentrism.

Although some courts and social welfare analysts are very supportive of claims by lesbians and gay men for equal treatment, many professionals in these communities retain negative views of those with minority sexual orientations.

The U.S. legal system has increasingly played an important role in either ensuring or denying the rights of people whose lives are affected by their sexual orientation (Flaks, 1994; Guggenheim, Lowe Dylan, & Curtis, 1996; Pollack, 1995; Rivera, 1987; Stein, 1996). Issues affected by the legal system and individual laws of states include:

- parents seeking child custody or visitation rights,
- gay men and lesbians seeking the right to be recognized as legal parents through adoption,
- states that ban gay men and lesbians from being foster or adoptive parents, and
- child welfare agencies' policies based on recognition of same-gendered couple benefits, a child's right to protection from harm while in state custody, and minor consent-to-treatment issues.

This chapter reviews the issues and uses individual and organizational case data to analyze the role that the law plays in the lives of children and families who are affected by issues of sexual orientation.

Family Law Issues Involving Children

In the United States, lesbian and gay children, youth, and families are denied most of the rights afforded to nongay children, youth, and families. Less than one-third of states offer full civil rights legal protection to gay and lesbian people. Courts routinely refuse to provide gay and lesbian relationships the legal recognition they need and deserve and often go so far as to treat lesbian and gay families with contempt. All family law issues are governed by state law. As such, most court cases are argued on a state-by-state basis, sometimes even court by court. This requires that litigation on these issues must occur again and again in state after state. Each victory has particular importance in the large struggle to gain full legal recognition for lesbian and gay children, youth, and families in every state.

Gay and lesbian children, youth, and families face many social and legal obstacles in the areas of child protection, family support, and out-of-home placement, and most clearly with respect to gay and lesbian parenting (T. Sullivan, 1994). The following examination evaluates the effect of the law concerning parenting by gay men and lesbians in several areas: custody and visitation, adoption and foster parenting, second-parent adoption, and issues related to procreation and parenting.

Custody and Visitation

Custody cases often arise involving lesbians and gay parents and their children. It is useful to distinguish between three types of custody and visitation disputes: those between a child's birthparents, those between a legal parent and a nonparent, and those that result in termination of parental rights with respect to the child. Courts employ different standards in each of these settings. In disputes between birthparents, the courts are required to determine custody and visitation on the basis of the "best interest of the child" (Goldstein, Solnit, Goldstein, & Freud, 1996; N. Hunter & Polikoff, 1976; Kleber, Howell, & Tibbits-Kleber, 1986). Laws governing disputes between legal parents and nonparents vary from state to state, but generally a presumption exists in favor of granting custody to the child's legal parent (Polikoff, 1986). In cases that lead to termination of parental rights with respect to the child, regardless of the parties involved, all states preserve the parent's rights unless the parent is found unfit or continuation of the relationship would be harmful to the child (Goldstein et al., 1996).

Regarding disputes between birthparents, many lesbians and gay men are the parents of children born to them from heterosexual unions. In some cases, when a child's nongay parent discovers that the other parent is gay or lesbian, he or she may attempt to limit the parenting role of the lesbian mother or gay father; challenges have also been brought by other relatives or government agencies. In these cases,* the sexual orientation of the lesbian or gay parent is often used to foment prejudice—to insinuate myths and stereotypes about gay or lesbian parents to provoke a denial of visitation or custody.

In general, the legal standards applied to child custody and visitation cases are vague. Because courts award custody based on the standard of the best interest of the child, courts frequently consider the parent's sexual orientation to be relevant to the child's best interest, and several courts have used the best interest

---

* The highly publicized Sharon Bottoms story, in which a lesbian mother lost custody of her daughter to a grandparent, epitomizes the double standards and outright heterocentrism facing gay and lesbian parents in many state courts. The antigay standards used to judge this Virginia mother's fitness as a parent represents a minority view among state courts.

standard to deny custody to gay and lesbian parents (Raymond, 1992). These laws vary from state to state depending on existing laws and statutes, and they usually vest a great deal of discretion in the judge.

Some states have created irrefutable presumptions against granting custody to a gay or lesbian parent. Other states have rebuttable presumptions that require a gay or lesbian parent to prove that his or her sexual orientation will not harm the child. Courts in at least 10 states have held that they will not deny custody to a parent on the grounds of sexual orientation absent proof that the parent's sexual orientation would adversely affect the child. Most courts have adopted an approach known as the "nexus approach," which requires a clear demonstration that the parent's sexual orientation actually causes harm to a child before it is deemed relevant. Under this approach, legal experts claim, the child's best interest become, and remains the proper focus of the case (Ferrero, Freker, & Foster, 2005; Lambda Legal Defense and Education Fund, 1996, 1997). As of May 1995, 29 states have adopted some variant of a nexus test. As of this writing, several localities have explicit laws guaranteeing that sexual orientation by itself cannot be used as a factor in determining custody or visitation (Lambda Legal Defense and Education Fund, 1997, pp. 2–3; M. Peguese, personal communication, February 4, 1999).

Moral issues frequently come into play. Some courts treat a parent's sexual orientation as determinative despite the statutory requirement that custody decisions be based on the child's overall best interest. Court that deny custody or restrict visitation by a gay or lesbian parent typically use one or more of five rationales to conclude that granting custody or unrestricted visitation to such a parent is not in the child's best interest. The first rationale is that the child will be harassed or ostracized (*Jacobson v. Jacobson*, 1981). Second is the fear that the child might become gay or lesbian (*J.L.P.[H]) v. D.J.P.*, 1982). Third, courts believe that living with or visiting a gay or lesbian parent may harm the child's moral well-being (*Roe v. Roe*, 1985). Fourth, they worry about child molestation (*J.L.P.[H]) v. D.J.P.*, 1982). Finally, they point to state sodomy statutes that they claim embody a state interest against homosexuality (*Constant A. v. Paul C.A.*, 1985; Verhovek, 1997; Williams, 1997).

In fact, none of these reasons are sufficiently related to the child's best interest to justify denying custody or restricting visitation by a gay or lesbian parent. Furthermore, none of these fears are borne out or supported by evidence (Dunlap, 1996; Patterson, 1994, 1995, 1996). All research to date has reached the same unequivocal conclusions about gay and lesbian parenting: The children of lesbian and gay parents grow up as successfully as the children of heterosexual parents (Elovitz, 1995). The next chapter, which focuses on research, will thoroughly review these issues.

A judge's view of the child's moral well-being may not be the same as the child's best interest. Although it is difficult to definitively state what beliefs regarding sexual orientation are best for the child, judges should avoid legislating their own sense of morality through custody decisions.

The court's fear that gay men and lesbians will molest their children is also not borne out in research (Groth & Birnbaum, 1978; Herek, 1991; Jenny et al., 1994; Newton, 1978). The majority of child molesters are heterosexually oriented men. Women, regardless of sexual orientation, rarely molest children. If courts were to make custody decisions based solely on the risk of molestation, they would probably award custody to the mother whether or not she was a lesbian ("Sexual Orientation and the Law," 1989, p. 130).

On June 26, 2003, the U.S. Supreme Court ruled 5 to 3, with Justice Kennedy writing the majority opinion, that Texas's "Homosexual Conduct" law is unconstitutional. This ruling effectively strikes down the sodomy laws in every state that still had them, 13 in all—but its effect is even broader. It has become a powerful tool for gay people in all 50 states where gay men and lesbians continue fighting to be treated equally. Sodomy laws criminalized oral and anal sex by consenting gay couples and, in some states, heterosexual couples, but courts used them almost exclusively to justify discrimination against lesbians and gay men. The Supreme Court heard two constitutional issues in Lambda Legal's case—whether the Texas law violated the Constitution's right to privacy and also whether it violated the Constitution's guarantee that all Americans will be treated equally under the law. The ruling focused on the first argument and established, for the first time, that lesbians and gay men have fundamental privacy rights.

The decision overturns the Supreme Court's 1986 ruling in *Bowers v. Hardwick*. In that decision—which was laced with antigay language and has been used against gay people in most civil rights cases since—the court upheld Georgia's sodomy law in a case brought by a man who was arrested while having consensual sex in his home with another man.

In the majority opinion, Justice Kennedy wrote, "*Bowers* was not correct when it was decided, and it is not correct today." The opinion also says:

> When sexuality finds overt expression in intimate conduct with another person, the conduct can be but one element in a personal bond that is more enduring. The liberty protected by the Constitution allows homosexual persons the right to make this choice.

The ruling closed the door on an era of intolerance and ushered in a new era of respect and equal treatment for gay Americans, and it recognizes that love, sexuality, and family play the same role in gay people's lives as they do in everyone else's.

The Texas 14th Court of Appeals, sitting *en banc*, earlier upheld the state's same-sex sodomy prohibition under the state and federal constitutions. The court's majority disagreed with a decision by its three-judge panel, which had found that the law violated the rights of the two men arrested at home for private, consensual sex. That panel had held that the Homosexual Conduct law violated the men's right to equal protection under the Texas Equal Rights Amendment by criminalizing conduct between same-sex partners but leaving the identical conduct legal for different-sex couples. On rehearing, the full court held that the law does not violate the right to equal treatment under the laws or to privacy from government prying into intimate adult conduct.

Lambda Legal petitioned the Texas Court of Criminal Appeals seeking further review of this unconstitutional law. Lambda Legal argued that the Homosexual Conduct law unfairly targets all lesbian and gay Texans for criminal condemnation and stigma and should be struck down once and for all. When that court—the state's highest court for appealing a criminal conviction—refused to hear the case, Lambda Legal (2003) asked the U.S. Supreme Court to hear its appeal.

Finally, the state's desire to promote policies underlying its sodomy statue is not a statutorily permissible predicate for a custody denial or visitation restriction, because it is irrelevant to the child's best interests. Moreover, because most state sodomy statutes prohibit opposite-gender as well as same-gender sodomy, these statutes cannot justify custody denials to only gay men and lesbians. Most courts who have denied custody to gay men and lesbians have not heard evidence indicating that the gay or lesbian parent has violated the sodomy statutes or that the nongay parent has not.

Adoption and Foster Care

Each state has an obligation to protect the health and welfare of children. Adoption and foster care provide homes for children who cannot safely or should not live at home with their birthfamilies. Although other chapters will explore the psychosocial issues associated with gay men and lesbians creating families, this section explores the legal consequences of adoption and foster care.

Adoption terminates the rights and responsibilities of birthparents and vests them in an adoptive parent or parents. Adoptions are officially sanctioned through public or state-licensed private agencies or via private placement arrangements. Courts, guided by the child's best interest, must review all adoption petitions; in addition, the agency's consent is required for agency adoptions, and in most states, judges hearing private adoption petitions must consider agency or social worker recommendations.

No one knows exactly how many lesbian, gay, bisexual, or transgender (LGBT) parents are raising children in the United States, just as no one knows how many people are LGBT. Some human sexuality studies have found that 10% of people are LGBT; others, counting only those who self-identify, put the number at 3% to 4% of the population.

Numerous social scientists have developed estimates of how many LGBT parents exist by using one well-known population study, the National Health and Social Life Survey (Lauman, Gagnon, Michael, & Michaels, 1994):

- Based on the survey's estimates, 1 to 9 million children are being raised by gay parents. This means that 1% to 12% of all children are being raised by a gay parent.

- Eight percent of self-identified gay, lesbian, or bisexual people are parents or legal guardians of a child younger than 18 who lives in their home (Kaiser Family Foundation [2000] national study of 405 randomly selected, self-identified lesbians, gays, and bisexuals in fall 2000).

- Of gay people, 49% would like to have children someday (according to the Kaiser Family Foundation, 2000, study).

No estimates exist as to how many gay people are already adoptive or foster parents. It is up to each state to decide whether to allow lesbian and gay people to become licensed as adoptive or foster parents (Ferrero et al., 2005, p. 21). Twenty-two states and the District of Columbia have granted adoptions to gay and lesbian individuals as well as same-sex couples. (It should be noted, however, that in some of these states, they have been granted only in certain counties.) The states are: Alaska, California, Colorado, Connecticut, Delaware, Illinois, Maryland, Massachusetts, Michigan, Minnesota, New Hampshire, New Jersey, New Mexico, New York, Ohio, Oregon, Pennsylvania, Rhode Island, Tennessee, Vermont, Washington, and Wisconsin.

Florida is the only state that explicitly prohibits adoption by gay and lesbian individuals and same-sex couples. Mississippi prohibits same-sex couples from adoption. Utah forbids adoption by any unmarried cohabiting couple, thereby discriminating against same-sex couples.

Nebraska ban gays from being foster parents, and recently, Indiana, Texas, Tennessee, and South Carolina have considered similar statewide policies. (Some children are placed in "relative care," raised by birth or fictive relatives, but this is often an informal, nonlegal process; no legal guardianship is transferred from the birthparent to the relative who cares for the child. Nothing is known about how many gay men have become parents through these kinds of placements.) In response to the growing need to find permanent parents for children and youth in need of permanent homes, many states have moved toward safeguarding the interests of the children of lesbians and gay men by strengthening their legal relationships with their families (Smothers, 1997a, 1997b; Szymanski, 1997).

States often discriminate against gay couples who want to adopt as a couple, but will allow single gay men to adopt (although only Ohio has explicitly said that single gay men and lesbians are eligible to adopt). Usually, if a couple wants to co-parent an adopted child, one partner adopts the child first, and then the other partner asks a court to grant a second-parent or co-parent adoption. According to the American Civil Liberties Union's (2005) Gay Rights Project, at least 21 states have granted second-parent adoptions to gay parents, ensuring that their children can enjoy the benefits of having two legal parents.

Four states (California, Massachusetts, New Jersey, and Vermont) as well as the District of Columbia explicitly permit joint adoption by lesbian or gay couples. All of those states, plus New York and Illinois, have also established statewide recognition of second-parent adoption. Judges in at least 20 other states have awarded second-parent adoptions. A few of these states, like Alaska and Washington, have approved numerous second-parent adoptions, and it is generally believed that lesbian and gay people have a much better chance of adopting their partner's children in these states (Ferrero et al., 2005, p. 19). Many states have laws that discourage adoption by unmarried couples, and these laws are frequently used to discriminate against lesbian and gay couples.

In recent years, Vermont and California have passed state laws that establish legal recognition of same-gendered couples that greatly benefit their entire family. Both states offer many or all of the benefits and responsibilities that are available to heterosexual couples through marriage. These states are much more likely to recognize not only same-gendered couples, but also their families. Recognizing that lesbians and gay men can be good parents, many state agencies and courts now apply a "best interests of the child" standard to decide cases in which child custody or visitation are in question.

People discriminate against lesbian and gays on many levels of society, but nowhere can this be seen as clearly as in the denial of the state to allow couples to marry. The benefits bestowed on couples by virtue of entering into a legal bond of marriage are economic, legal, and emotional. These benefits are meant to support not only both partners, but also their children. Because lesbian and gay relationships are devalued and dismissed, families with children suffer from the fallout of not being legally recognized or of having to go through extra steps to gain such legal validation, such as second-parent adoptions. Regardless of these hurdles, many lesbian and gay men have successfully created families through foster parenting, adoption, and relative care options.

Some conservative states, led by "family values" ideologues who play on fear, ignorance, and uncertainty about the "gay lifestyle," use harmful stereotypes to scare others into believing that gay people should not be allowed to adopt a child or be a foster parent (see "Arizona Law," 1997; Arnold, 1997; Baldauf, 1997; "Court Refuses," 1997; "Florida Judge," 1997; Freiberg, 1999; "Georgia Ban," 1998; A. Green, 1999; J. Green, 1999; Johnsrude, 1997; Kessler, 1997; McFarland, 1998; Tanner, 1996).

Following the currents of tolerance and intolerance in the United States over the past 20 years is like watching a tennis match—the head starts to spin. As of 2006, Florida is the only state whose statutes explicitly prohibit adoption by a gay individual. Legislation introduced in 1999 in the New Hampshire legislature repealed the law banning gay men from becoming foster parents (St. Pierre, 1999). Gay and lesbian parenting is, at the time of this writing, under attack in Texas, Tennessee, and Indiana. Over the past three years, courts considered and defeated antigay adoption bans in Arkansas, Idaho, Indiana, Oklahoma, and Texas (Ferrero et al., 2005, p. 17). As acceptance of lesbians and gay men in North American culture has increased, attacks from the radical right have also increased (Hartman & Laird, 1998, p. 265; Hennie, 1999).

As ethical debates continue over the appropriateness of lesbians and gay men parenting children and youth, are we losing track of the point? The real issue is that children and youth need responsible, loving parents. We must keep in mind two vital points in this debate: First, sexual orientation is unrelated to whether someone is a good parent or not. Second, we are starting to see results of studies of gay and lesbian parenting that show that children in these families are as well-adjusted, happy, and successful as their counterparts raised in heterosexual-parented families (Patterson, 1996).

It is time that child welfare providers recognize and embrace the fact that some lesbians and gay men would be wonderful parents to children and youth who are in desperate need of permanent homes.

In contrast, foster care is intended to provide a temporary home for a child. Permanency planning mandates that after a period of no more than 18 months in foster care, a child will be either reunited with his or her birthfamily or freed for adoption. Many states, however, make it difficult for lesbians or gay men to be foster parents (Groninger, 1996). In Mississippi, for example, only married couples are allowed to be licensed as foster parents. In other states, although many child welfare agencies and social workers may be opposed to placement in gay or lesbian homes, such placements occur either because the social workers are unaware of the applicant's sexual orientation or because they unofficially recognize that the gay or lesbian applicant will provide a good home for the young person (Achtenberg, 1990; Kessler, 1997; Ricketts, 1991; Ricketts & Achtenberg, 1987, 1990; A. Sullivan, 1995).

Florida remains the only jurisdiction with statutory bans on the adoption of children by gay and lesbian people. Although the majority of states no longer officially deem lesbians and gay men as unfit to rear a child, each state decides independently who can adopt, and legislators continue to introduce bills barring adoptions and foster parenting by gay and lesbian people into state legislatures every year. In Arkansas, a regulation that would prohibit anyone from being a foster or adoptive parent if any adult member of the household is homosexual received approval from the governor-appointed Child Welfare Review Board (J. Green, 1999). Two bills have been proposed in Texas—one barring the state from placement of children in adoptive or foster homes in which "homosexual conduct is occurring or is likely to occur," and the other mandating the removal of children already placed with gay or lesbian foster parents. President George W. Bush, while governor of Texas, went on record as saying that he would sign a bill to ban lesbian and gay people seeking to become foster parents if it should come to his desk (Hennie, 1999, p. 1). In Utah, the head of the state's Division of Child and Family Services Board proposed a regulation to prohibit gay and unmarried couples from adopting, and in Indiana, an elected statewide official introduced a bill to prevent gay people from adopting or becoming foster parents (Freiberg, 1999).

Although openly gay and lesbian adoptions have occurred in a number of jurisdictions, including California, the District of Columbia, New Mexico, and Ohio, the most common practice is for a single individual to apply for adoption as the legal adopter of the child. Couples who desire joint custody then apply for a second-parent adoption, which the following section will explore.

Restrictions on the ability of gay men and lesbians to provide foster or adoptive homes for needy children run counter to the welfare of children needing such homes. States' and agencies' refusal to place children with gay men and lesbians are also sometimes based on the perceived potential harm to children, as discussed in the section on custody and visitation (i.e., fear of molestation, fear that the child will be stigmatized, and fear that the child will become gay or lesbian). Refusals to permit lesbians and gay men to adopt or become foster parents stems in part from a fear of appearing to accept gay people and same-gendered relationships to any degree, which resonates with the experience of heterocentrism.

Deciding whether a particular placement is in the child's best interest always should involve balancing that specific placement against other available alternatives (Goldstein et al., 1996). The benefits of placing a child in a gay or lesbian home are especially clear for hard-to-place children, and most self-identified gay and lesbian adolescents are, by virtue of their orientation, hard to place. Many states have a shortage of foster or adoptive parents; many children end up in inappropriate settings such as shelters, diagnostic centers, psychiatric hospitals, or congregate care institutions (Mallon, 1992) if they cannot find a home with the right fit. Because a permanent home is a requirement for all children and is critical to their development, gay and lesbian individuals and couples can provide a much needed source of potential foster and adoptive parents for such young people.

Because refusals to permit gay men or lesbians to become foster parents do not serve the affected children's best interests (Raymond, 1992), they can in some cases be challenged in court on that basis. In all states except Florida, a would-be foster or adoptive parent challenging a judge's refusal to grant a private placement adoption petition can argue that the denial does not serve the child's best interest. In other situations, however, such as denial of a foster care license or when an agency refuses to place a gay or lesbian individual or couple on its wait list, the would-be parent has no state law cause of action with which to challenge the denial.

Second-Parent Adoption

Until recently, in most lesbian- and gay-headed families, only one parent was recognized as the legal parent. Dissimilar from the traditional form of adoption, which recognizes only the parental right of the birthparent as the current legal parent, second-parent adoptions leave the parental rights of one legally recognized parent intact and create a second legally recognized parent for the child. Although second-parent adoption is currently the only way for gay and lesbian couples to both become legal parents of their children, it has also become a fairly routine means among children of nongay parents.

One of the first cases tested occurred in New York was the 1992 case *Matter of Adoption of Evan*. In this case, two women living together in a committed long-term relationship, which they perceived as permanent for 14 years, decided to have a child together. Pursuant to their joint plan, the women were alternatively inseminated with sperm obtained from a male friend who formally relinquished any parental rights to the child. When Evan was born, he lived with both women. They both participated in raising him over the following six years. Evan viewed both women as parents.

In considering Evan's best interests, the court evaluated homestudy reports that described the non-birthparent as loving, warm, and nurturing; as committed to Evan; and as an effective parent to him. Having concluded on the fact presented that the adoption was in Evan's best interest, the New York County Surrogates Court ultimately granted adoption to the non-birthmother.

A similar case, which was one of the most highly publicized changes in the area of child adoption laws for lesbian and gay couples, can be seen in the Massachusetts *Adoption of Tammy* case. By a 5 to 4 decision, after months of testimony attesting to the best interest of the child, the Supreme Judicial Court of Massachusetts upheld the adoption of the child by a lesbian couple who had raised her since birth.

In the *Matter of Jacob* (1995), the New York Court of Appeals ruled in a 4-3 decision that "the unmarried partner of a child's biological mother, whether heterosexual or homosexual, who is raising the child together with the biological parent, can become the child's second parent by means of adoption." The ruling established for all of New York state that the adoption code does permit second-parent adoption. Courts have made similar groundbreaking decisions in New Jersey (Smothers, 1997b; Szymanski, 1997). In October of 1997, Jon Holden-Galluccio and his partner, Michael Galluccio, challenged the New Jersey law that prevented same-gender couples and unmarried heterosexual couples from jointly adopting children, so they could adopt their child, Adam (at the time of this writing, now 4 years old), who had lived in their home as a foster child since 3 months old. Judge Sybil R. Moses of Superior Court in Bergen County, New Jersey, granted the joint adoption, saying that it was in the best interest of the child. Two months later, all legal barriers to joint adoption by unmarried same-gender and heterosexual unmarried couples were removed in a broader consent decree negotiated by the judge, state welfare officials, and attorneys with the Lesbian and Gay Rights Project of the Civil Liberties Union, who represented the men and several other gay couples. New Jersey became the first state to establish a policy treating gay and unmarried couples the same way it treats married couples regarding adoptions (Smothers, 1998, p. B5).

As of April 1997, second-parent adoptions by lesbian and gay couples have been approved by courts in the District of Columbia and 21 states. In most cases, the approvals were from lower-level courts (Lambda Legal, 1997, p. 6).

Issues Related to Procreation and Parenting

Gay men and lesbians are as capable of procreation as bisexuals or heterosexuals. Many gay men and lesbians are choosing to have children via alternative insemination, via surrogacy, or through sexual intercourse. Legally defining rights and responsibilities of the other birthparent and consideration of the rights of the co-parent are factors that legal experts and child welfare professionals must confront. Clearly, unless a child is adopted, his or her birthmother is the legal parent. Whether the father is the legal parent is more complicated and depends on the mother's marital status, the reproductive technique used, and applicable state statutes. If the child is conceived through sexual intercourse and paternity is established, the father generally has equal rights and responsibilities. If the child is conceived through intrauterine insemination, the donor's status depends on whether the state regulates intrauterine insemination of unmarried women. As with many family law issues, laws governing donor insemination vary from state to state, and most states' laws apply only to married women, which excludes lesbians. Some states do not have any laws that govern insemination. A majority of states have some form of legal protection for the lesbian mother, provided that the insemination was performed in a doctor's office (Bernfeld, 1995; Lambda Legal, 1997).

Although donor insemination requires virtually no medical expense and can be performed at home without any involvement by state officials or medical professionals, it is not without legal risks.

When a lesbian or gay couple chooses to have a child, only the birthparent is automatically the child's legal parent. If the legal parent dies, the surviving partner, or co-parent, could lose custody to the child's other birthparent or to other relatives of the child, especially grandparents. In addition, if the couple separates, the legal parent may be able to prohibit contact between the co-parent and the child.

Same-gendered couples can attempt to avoid these difficulties in several ways. They could file for second-parent adoption, ensuring that both partners have equal rights and responsibilities with respect to the child. The birthparent could appoint the co-parent as testamentary guardian in the case of the birthparent's death. Finally, if the couple separates or the birthparent dies without specifically implying guardianship, the co-parent could claim custody or visitation rights under the "psychological parent" theory (Goldstein et al., 1996, p. 90).*

The infamous *Baby M* (1988) case in New Jersey brought the legal and ethical complexity of surrogacy to light. This particular case, involving Mary Beth

---

* A psychological parent is an adult who, regardless of biological relationship to the child, on a continuing day-to-day basis fulfills the child's psychological need for a parent, as well as the child's physical needs.

Whitehead, who contracted with William Stern and his wife to bear a child, was a media event and a lighting rod for both sides of the surrogacy issue. Surrogacy agreements are one means by which gay men are opting to create families. Surrogacy arrangements, as Martin (1993) noted, are "contracts for the sale of reproductive services" (p. 166). Surrogacy as a means of parenting is so new that the legal issues are still confusing and at times conflicting. In Arizona, surrogacy is illegal; in Kentucky, Michigan, and Utah, it is illegal only if a woman is paid to bear a child. Regardless, an important distinction exists between statues that criminalize surrogacy and those that do not automatically uphold surrogacy contracts. If all parties involved in a surrogacy arrangement are satisfied, there is usually nothing to worry about. Legal problems arise when the surrogate mother either changes her mind and keeps the child, or when the birthfather is unwilling to accept the child once it is born. The major legal hurdle for a gay father with respect to surrogacy is to establish that he is the legal father of the child and to enforce the mother's contractually stated intention to surrender her parental rights.

Conclusions

This chapter has introduced the reader to the role that the law plays in child welfare services for people affected by issues of sexual orientation. Court decisions, legal actions, and legislation frame the discussion concerning the rights of gay and lesbian children and adolescents, adoptive parents, and birthparents. Child welfare practitioners and policymakers must work in collaboration with attorneys and others in the legal professions to ensure that people affected by issues of sexual orientation are treated justly and equitably.

For many years, it was almost impossible for a person to be gay or lesbian and rear a child, but in today's Western society, gay men and lesbians are raising children and involved in the lives of children in many ways. Some are their children from heterosexual marriages; others are adopted or foster children. An increasing number of gay men and lesbians are choosing to create children by alternative insemination, surrogacy, and heterosexual intercourse. Regardless of the circumstances of the child's birth, the legal treatment of the parent/child relationship should not rest solely on the parent's sexual orientation. Rather than promoting prejudicial attitudes based solely on decisions made based on false stereotypes or perceived environmental intolerance, courts, legal experts, legislatures, and social workers should instead focus on the need for a stable home and a supportive environment for children.

In the United States, lesbian and gay people are denied most of the rights afforded to nongay people due to dominant heterocentric societal attitudes. Courts routinely refuse to provide gay and lesbian relationships with the legal recognition they need and deserve. As this chapter has argued, because sexual orientation alone is irrelevant to parenting ability, gay men and lesbians should not be denied custody or visitation with their children, or the possibility of becoming adoptive or foster parents. Second-parent adoptions and other parenting issues related to alternative procreation techniques are also important areas for social workers to develop their knowledge base to effectively work with gay and lesbian children, youth, and families affected by issues of sexual orientation.

Some glimmers of hope exist, however, to show that things are changing for lesbian- and gay-headed families. Two recent examples should be noted. A Maryland judge, M. Brooke Murdock of Baltimore City Circuit Court, struck down a state law banning same-sex marriage, saying the measure violated a state constitutional amendment prohibiting sex discrimination (Liptak, 2006). Judge Murdock relied on a 1967 decision by the U.S. Supreme Court, *Loving v. Virginia*, which struck down bans on interracial marriages. Judge Murdock wrote further that "the court is not unaware of the dramatic impact of its ruling." But she rejected all the arguments offered in favor of the law, among them that children are best served by one male parent and one female parent.

"Prevention of same-sex marriage," Judge Murdock wrote, "is not rationally related to the state's interests in promoting stable families and protecting the best interests of children." "Tradition and social values alone cannot support adequately a discriminatory statutory classification," she added. "When tradition is the guise under which prejudice or animosity hides, it is not a legitimate state interest."

In another case, Virginia legislators recently rejected a bill that would undermine a court decision allowing gay and lesbian couples who adopt Virginia-born children to be listed on state-issued birth certificates.

Since the court ruling this past spring, the Virginia Health Department's Division of Vital Records and Health Statistics has issued about nine birth certificates to same-sex couples, an official at the department said. The challenge to Virginia's policy was brought by three same sex couples: two in the District of Columbia, and one in New York. The couples adopted Virginia-born children through courts in other states that allowed same-sex couples to adopt. The couples could not get new Virginia birth certificates, which are issued by the state of birth (T. Smith, 2006).

Gay and lesbian people have increasingly gained in visibility and public acceptance during the latter part of the 20th century, but for the most part, the lesbian and gay community has existed in a parallel world—separate and apart from mainstream culture, not by their own choosing, but because they have been deterred from full protection because of intolerant societal attitudes. The next frontier requires that gay and lesbian people continue to lead the way out of the closet, becoming skilled at using legal means to achieve not special rights, but full and equal rights as protected by the law and the Constitution in the same areas in which heterosexual people and families are guaranteed corresponding protection.

CHAPTER 4

RESEARCH ON LESBIAN AND GAY PARENTING

ALTHOUGH A NUMBER OF CONSERVATIVE POLITICIANS have noted that "studies show" that children are better off with a mother and a father, they are in fact referring to studies that compared children of two-parent heterosexual couples with those of single, presumably, heterosexual mothers. The findings of these studies do suggest that children are better off in two-parent families, but what they do not suggest is anything about sexual orientation, which was not measured or even considered. As Shuster (2005) noted in quoting Charlotte Patterson (1992, 1994, 1995, 1996), the best-known researcher on issues of sexual orientation and parenting, these studies "don't have anything to do with sexual orientation, and are therefore irrelevant to the question about how 'children fare' in households headed by lesbian and gay parents" (p. 14).

But what do we know about how children and youth fare in households headed by lesbians and gay men? This chapter will review the existing research to provide an overview of the evidence on the effects on children with lesbian or gay parents. It will then use the research findings to examine (and dispel) the myths and facts about gay men and lesbians as parents and recommend future directions for research.

Research Limitations

The nature and scope of research studies on lesbian and gay families continues to grow. The earliest documentation on lesbian mothers and gay fathers (Bozett, 1980; Osman, 1972) was mostly explored in the context of children born in heterosexual marriages that ended in divorce. Such early studies have been replaced by those focusing on children in planned lesbian- and gay-headed families without the con-

45

founding variable of divorces and the coming-out process of the parents. As with all research projects, some limitations to the research in the area of lesbian and gay parenting exist. Because not all lesbians and gay men are "out," random representative sampling of lesbian and gay parents is a challenge to methods. This is particularly so as no reliable data exist on the number and whereabouts of lesbian or gay parents in the general population in the United States or elsewhere.

The existing, limited research has biases toward white, urban, well-educated, and mature lesbian mothers and gay fathers, and relatively small samples are recruited through community networks. It is not easy to define groups that would be appropriate comparisons with lesbians or gay parents—and comparing them with a heterosexual parenting population does not lend greater legitimacy either, as intrinsic differences exist. Some recient studies (Golombok et al. 2003; Wainright and Patterson, 2006) which have utilized larger representative sample populations report finding the same result as previous studies, that children and youth reared by a lesbian or gay parent develop much in the same ways as do children and youth living with different-gendered parents.

While heterosexual parenting research and gay/lesbian parenting comparison research confirms that there are no disadvantages associated with being reared by a lesbian or gay parent, that's not to say that gay/lesbian and heterosexual parent families are identical. Researchers have identified some differences, but none that negatively affect a child's adjustment.

How are lesbian- and gay-headed families different from heterosexual families? One of the most consistent findings over the past 10 years, according to Patterson (1996), is that same-gendered couples with and without children tend to establish a more even distribution of household tasks compared with heterosexual couples. Without socially prescribed guidance on gendered roles, lesbian and gay parents tend to value equality in partnership and structure an equitable division of labor in housework, childrearing, and work outside the home. Although this repeated finding seems to be well known in the mental health community, it is has not been discussed in the mainstream dialogue about the pros and cons of lesbian and gay marriage or parenting. The challenge for social services professionals, especially those recruiting, assessing, and supporting lesbian and gay foster and adoptive homes, is to understand what this finding might mean for the children and their parents.

Stacey and Biblarz (2001) identified parental gender to be predictive of parenting skill. All mothers (heterosexual, lesbian, birth, and adoptive) are more likely than fathers to be more invested in and skilled at caring for children. Therefore, when two women co-parent, gender and sexual orientation interact, with two mothers both committed to and working together toward creating an equitable and mutually caring environment that provides a loving and supportive foundation for their child's developing self-esteem. This may be explained by the fact that women tend to have greater parenting skills because they tend to spend more time at being primary parents than do most men. When men are primary caregivers, such as the gay dads interviewed by Mallon (2004), they have high parenting skills too.

The research on gay birthfathers and their children is extremely limited. No studies in the literature have systematically examined the effect of fathers' sexual identity on their children. Two studies (McPherson, 1993; Sbordone, 1993) show similar parenting styles and skills between gay and heterosexual fathers. Mallon's (2004) study of the parenting process in a group of 20 self-identified gay fathers found they were more likely to endorse a nurturing role for fathers, less likely to emphasize the importance of economic support, and less likely to show affection to their partner in front of the children (Barret & Robinson, 2000; Bigner & Jacobsen, 1992). Further results indicate that gay fathers are as effective as heterosexual fathers in caring for their children. They have been shown to be more consistent in limit setting with their children than are heterosexual fathers. They have also been found to be more emotionally expressive and nurturing with their children, less likely to prioritize their "breadwinner" functions over their parenting roles, and less interested in conventional gender-role behaviors than heterosexual fathers (Mallon, 2004).

Fears About Lesbian and Gay Parents

Although a wealth of literature about gay and lesbian parenting has existed since the mid-1980s (Benkov, 1994; Bigner, 1996; Bigner & Jacobsen, 1989a, 1989b; Bozett, 1987; Martin, 1993; McGarry, 2004; Mitchell, 1996; Muzio, 1993, 1996; Pies, 1985), the idea of a lesbian or gay man as a primary nurturing figure rearing children is still remarkable to many (Mallon, 2004). Many social work professionals still hold firm to a belief system grounded in the ubiquitous, negative myths and stereotypes about lesbians and gay men (Mallon, 1999a)—for example, that a lesbian or gay man might abuse children, that children might be encouraged or "recruited" to be gay or lesbian, or that lesbians and gay men are not suitable role models.

Those who oppose the idea of gay men and lesbians as parents base their thinking on a number of fears, for example, that:

- the child will be bullied or ostracized because of having lesbian or gay parents,

- the child might become gay or lesbian because of having a lesbian or gay parental role model,
- living with or having contact with a gay or lesbian parent may harm the child's moral well-being (these beliefs may have their foundation in religious texts that condemn homosexuality), or
- the child will be abused (based on the myth that all gay men are sexual predators).

None of these rationales are borne out or supported by evidence (Carey, 2005; Dunlap, 1996; Patterson, 1996; Stacey & Biblarz, 2001). Crucially, such attitudes can affect social work professionals undertaking homestudy assessments of lesbians and gay men.

The myth of gay men as child abusers (Groth, 1978; Newton, 1978) remains ingrained in the psyche of many people, including professionals in the social work field, so much so that the idea that gay men would be allowed to parent seems, to some, incredulous. These ideas derive from the cultural myth that men in general, and gay men in particular, are sexual predators, unable to control themselves sexually and prone to sexualize all situations.

The published social science literature (Cramer, 1986; Groth, 1978; Groth & Birnbaum, 1978; Herek, 1991; Newton, 1978) also confirms that the myth of child abuse by gay men is a fallacy. Pedophilia is the attraction of an adult to children for sexual gratification and has nothing to do with the sexual orientation of the perpetrator. The most recent study examining sexual orientation and child sexual abuse (Jenny et al., 1994), which looked at 269 cases of sexually abused children, found that only two offenders were identified as gay. These findings suggest that a child's risk of being sexually abused by the heterosexual partner of a relative is more than 100 times greater than the risk of being abused by somebody who might be identifiable as being gay, bisexual, or lesbian.

Quality of Family Relations

Numerous studies show that the qualities that make good fathers, mothers, or foster parents are universal and not related to sexual orientation or gender. The need for parental involvement in the lives of their children has been very clearly established by many (Lamb, 1986, 1987, 1997). The ability to love and care for a child is not determined by one's sexual orientation (A. Sullivan, 1995). Furthermore, the desire to parent is not exclusive to heterosexuals, but is one shared by many lesbians and gay men (Benkov, 1994; Frommer, 1996; J. Green, 1999; Mallon, 2004; Martin, 1993; Savage, 1999; Shernoff, 1996).

According to the meta-analysis of the relevant research spanning two decades conducted by Stacey and Biblarz (2001), none of the significant differences in parenting as reported in the research apply to children's self-esteem, psychological well-being, or social adjustment, nor were there differences in parents' self-esteem, mental health, or commitment to their children. In other words, although differences exist, the research did not identify them as deficits. In fact, the studies found no negative effects of lesbian and gay parenting

A few studies reported some differences that could represent advantages of lesbian parenting. For example, several studies found that lesbian co-mothers share family responsibilities more equally than heterosexual married parents, and some research hints that children benefit from egalitarian co-parenting. A few studies found that lesbians worry less than heterosexual parents about the gender conformity of their children. Perhaps that helps to account for a few studies that found that sons of lesbians play less aggressively and that children of lesbians communicate their feelings more freely, aspire to a wider range of occupations, and score higher on self-esteem. Most professionals would see these differences as positive elements, but some critics of these studies have misrepresented these differences as evidence that the children are suffering from gender confusion.

Finally, some studies reported that lesbian mothers feel more comfortable discussing sexuality with their children and accepting their children's sexuality—whatever it might be. More to the point are data reported in a 25-year British study (Golombok & Tasker, 1996). Few of the young adults in this study identified themselves as gay or lesbian, but a larger minority of those with lesbian mothers did report that they were more open to exploring their sexuality and had at one time or another considered or actually had a same-sex relationship.

The Golombok and Tasker (1996) longitudinal study of children brought up in lesbian households assessed the quality of mother-child interaction (primary older children). The researchers found that children with lesbian mothers had closer relationships with their mothers and were more likely to have a secure attachment style than those in a heterosexual family comparison group. As young adults, the respondents reported being able to communicate well with their mother about their own relationships more than did those in the comparison group. Golombok, Tasker, and Murray (1997) found similar results in a later study examining family relationships and the socioemotional development of children of lesbian and single heterosexual mothers.

Similarly, Chan, Raboy, and Patterson (2000) noted that as far as the quality of family relationships is concerned, research comparing various forms of lesbian and heterosexual families provides consistent evidence that children are more powerfully affected by *how* family members relate to each other than by family structure or parental sexual orientation.

Most children brought up in planned, lesbian-led families and by lesbian mothers who had a previous heterosexual relationship have regular contact with adults beyond their immediate household, including grandparents, other relatives, and male and female family friends (Golombok, Spencer, & Rutter, 1983; Patterson, Hurt, & Mason, 1998).

Although most research to date on gay and lesbian parenting is based on those who are birthparents, researchers looking at gay and lesbian adoptive and foster parents have reached the same unequivocal conclusions. That is, the children of lesbian and gay parents grow up as successfully as the children of heterosexual parents (Bos et al, 2004; Golombok et al., 1983, 2003; Patterson, 1994, 1995, 1996; Tasker & Golombok, 1997; Bronston, 2004; Vanfraussen, K., Ponjaert-Kristofferson, I. & Brewaeys, A., 2002, 2003; Wainright & Patterson, 2006; Wainright, Russell, & Patterson, 2004).

Since 1980, more than 20 studies conducted and published in the United States, Australia, and the United Kingdom have addressed the way parental sexual orientation affects children. Another meta-analysis of 18 such studies concluded that:

> The results demonstrate no differences on any measures between the heterosexual and homosexual parents regarding parenting styles, emotional adjustment, and sexual orientation of the child(ren). (Allen & Burrell, 1996, p. 19)

Not one study has found that the children of lesbian or gay parents face greater social stigma. No evidence supports the belief that the children of gay parents are more likely to be abused or to suggest that the children of these parents are more likely to be gay or lesbian themselves. Children will, in fact, be who they are. It is important to bear in mind that the majority of lesbians and gay men have been raised by heterosexual parents.

Becoming a Parent: Making Decisions

Two studies stand out as seminal works on adoption and fostering from a British perspective: Skeates and Jabri's (1988) groundbreaking *Fostering and Adoption by Lesbians and Gay Men* and Hicks and McDermott's (1999) *Lesbian and Gay Fostering and Adoption*.

Although lesbians and gay men become foster parents and adoptive parents for some of the same reasons as heterosexuals, they have some unique circumstances as well (Mallon, 1999b, 2004; Pies, 1990). Unlike their heterosexual counterparts, gay or lesbian individuals and couples who wish to parent will have to give more careful consideration to how they will become a parent and at the outset will be open to different ways of becoming a family and parenting children, for example through adoption and fostering (Ricketts, 1991; Ricketts & Achtenberg, 1990), surrogacy, or donor insemination (Bernfeld, 1995).

Lesbians or gay men who choose to foster or adopt as single parents will face stresses more to do with single parenting than with their sexuality (Feigelman & Silverman, 1997; Groze & Rosenthal, 1991; Marindin, 1997; Melina, 1998, p. 292).

On the positive side, gay men and lesbians who choose to create families have the advantage of redefining and reinventing their own meaning for family and parenting, precisely because they exist outside of the traditionally defined "family." They have the unique opportunity to break out of preconceived gender roles and be a new kind of father or mother to a child (Benkov, 1994). Most lesbians and gay men who parent are not invested in raising gay or lesbian children as suggested by some, but in raising children who will be authentic and supporting their children regardless of their expressions of gender or sexual orientation.

Future Research

Although new research on gay and lesbian adoption and foster partenting is being published even as this book is in press (Craig-Olsen, Craig, & Morton, 2006; Downs & James, 2006; Matthews & Cramer, 2006) the field needs a study on adoptive parents that compares children adopted by lesbian and gay parents with children adopted by heterosexual parents. To my knowledge, no such study has yet been undertaken. A need also exists for more research on gay fathers and for studies that include gay fathers who have children through surrogacy or other means. It is also critical that research studies should have a more diverse representation of lesbian and gay parents in terms of ethnicity, race, education, income, and nationality.

Myths Versus Facts

Myth: The only acceptable home for a child is one with a mother and father who are married to each other.

> *Fact:* Research shows that children thrive in many different types of family structure. The United States has increasingly more diverse types of families, as discussed in the introduction.

Myth: Children need a mother and a father to have proper male and female role models.

> *Fact:* Children get their role models from many places besides their parents. These include grandparents, aunts and uncles, teachers, friends, and neighbors.

Myth: Gay men and lesbians do not have stable relationships and would not know how to be good parents.

Fact: Many lesbians and gay men are in stable, committed relationships, and many are successfully involved in the parenting of children. All of the evidence shows that lesbians and gay men can and do make good parents. (To further dispel this myth, see Freeman, 2005; Harris, 2005; "What We Think," 2005 and " Okay With It," 2005.)

Myth: Children raised by gay or lesbian parents are more likely to grow up gay themselves.

Fact: All of the available evidence demonstrates that the sexual orientation of parents has no effect on the sexual orientation of their children and that children of lesbian and gay parents are no more likely than any other child to grow up to be gay. In fact, most lesbians and gay men have been raised by heterosexual parents. Of course, some children of lesbians and gay men will grow up to be gay, as will some children of heterosexual parents. These children will have the added advantage of being raised by parents who are supportive and accepting of their sexuality. Some evidence shows that children of gays and lesbians are more tolerant and open to difference.

Myth: Children raised by gay or lesbian parents will be subjected to bullying and may be rejected by their peers.

Fact: Children make fun of other children for all kinds of reasons: for being too short or too tall, for being too thin or too fat, or for being of a different race or religion. Children can show remarkable resilience, especially if they have a stable, loving home environment and parents who can support them. Because of the homophobia that exists in society, some children will experience discrimination and negative comments for having lesbian or gay parents. Social workers need to acknowledge and address this, and they need to give children the strategies and supports necessary to deal with these experiences.

Myth: Gay men are more likely to abuse children.

Fact: There is no connection between homosexuality and pedophilia. All of the legitimate scientific evidence supports this assertion. In addition to the research mentioned previously (Jenny et al., 1994), of the cases studied involving sexual abuse of boys by men, 74% of the abusers were or had been in a heterosexual relationship with the boy's mother or another female relative.

Myth: Children raised by gay men or lesbians will be brought up in an immoral environment.

Fact: The research by Cameron, Cameron, and Landess (1996) is most frequently cited to support the claim that having a lesbian or gay parent adversely affects children. They proposed that homosexuality is a "learned pathology" that parents pass on to their children by "modelling, seduction and contagion." Ample evidence discounts this "research": The authors have been denounced by the American Sociological Association (ASA) for willfully misrepresenting research; Paul Cameron was expelled from the American Psychiatric Association and censored by ASA for unethical scholarly practices, such as making selective, misleading representations of research and making claims that could not be substantiated. Nonetheless, as Stacey and Biblarz (2001) noted, bias against gay and lesbian parenting remains sufficiently strong for this work to continue to be cited in court cases and policy hearings.

Conclusion

This chapter has focused solely on the evidence in relation to lesbians and gay men *choosing* parenthood and the effects on the children they parent. Adoption and fostering, as is so well stated by Scott (2002):

> Are not "gay rights issues"; the "rights" they involve are the rights of children and youth to safe and effective care, and the evidence from research is that this is no less likely to be the case where parents are lesbians or gay men. (p. 15)

The body of literature on this topic is nascent and relatively homogeneous. Numerous authors reviewing the research relevant to lesbian and gay fostering and adoption have concluded that no evidence exists that lesbians and gay men are less capable of being effective parents than heterosexuals (Brooks & Goldberg, 2001; Hicks, 2000; Stacey & Biblarz, 2001). Although researchers should certainly undertake more research specific to the fostering and adoption experience, a foundation of evidence indicates that the sexual orientation of parents makes very little difference to outcomes for children.

Although the research findings summarized here are highly relevant to the concerns raised by those opposed to the consideration of lesbians and gay men as potential foster parents or adoptive parents, further research into the specific experiences of children so fostered and adopted is clearly needed.

As social work practitioners, particularly those working to recruit, assess, and support lesbian and gay parents interested in fostering or adopting, it is essential for us to read the research and to analyze, interpret, and discuss the findings. It is incumbent upon us as a professional community to be clear about the facts, to be able to rebut the misinformation presented by those who may not see lesbians and gay men as appropriate resources for children in need of homes, and to nurture the narratives of truth that we have witnessed through case examples. Research findings and their interpretation have enormous effects in many influential arenas, including court cases for custody and visiting rights; for judges, child advocates, and professionals in the physical and mental health communities; and for those charged with developing and enacting legislation that guides our laws. In the midst of a politically charged environment in which negative stereotypes and ideological assertions can easily gain status as truth, it is essential for social work practitioners in the child welfare field to become familiar with what is known and not known from the research studies so that lesbian and gay potential parents can be recruited, assessed, and supported by informed and competent practitioners.

CHAPTER 5

ISSUES FOR LESBIANS AND GAY MEN WHEN CONSIDERING PARENTING

THE FOCUS OF THIS CHAPTER IS the issues that lesbians and gay men face as they make the decision to become parents and their experiences as adopters and foster parents. The chapter is based on an analysis of the existing literature, qualitative data analysis from interviews conducted with lesbians and gay men who have engaged in fostering or adopting, and more than 31 years of clinical practice experience.

As lesbians and gay men are becoming more visible in U.S. society, agencies are considering them more seriously as potential adoptive or foster parents. The increasing number of lesbians and gay men choosing to adopt or become foster parents has brought the issue of gay and lesbian parenting to the forefront of the field of children, youth, and family services. Social work practitioners need to consider a number of issues to develop a knowledge base that will lead to competent practice with lesbian and gay parents.

First, it is important to recognize that although many similarities exist, lesbian- and gay-parented families also differ from the heterosexually parented family. The conventional notion of a family presumes that it will include two parents, one of each gender, that they will share a loving relationship and live under one roof, that they will both be biologically related to the children they raise, and that they will be recognized legally as a family. This mom-and-dad nuclear family is the baseline model in Western culture against which all other models of family are measured, and it is assumed by most to be the optimal family environment for child development, compared to which all other types of families are viewed as deficient in some way.

This model, however, does not apply to families with a lesbian or gay parent. In families with a lesbian or gay couple, usually at least one parent has no biological relationship to the child. These families almost always have a parent child relationship not recognized or protected by the law.

We need to accept the premise that it is quality of care, and not the composition of the family system, that determines what is optimal for children's healthy development. The ability of lesbian and gay parents to provide for the social and emotional health of their children just as adequately as heterosexual parents has been documented repeatedly in the research literature and outlined in Chapter 3. We must also examine our own notion of family and further learn to identify what constitutes family based on the loving bonds of responsibility that have been both intended and fulfilled, and not solely on biological, legal, or conventional definitions.

Decision to Explore Parenting

I have always loved children, and there has always been a part of me that wanted to be a dad. As a gay man, I thought it was impossible—who was going to let me be someone's parent? And it wasn't like I could just go out and get pregnant myself and have a baby. I guess I had internalized a lot of the homophobia that I had been fed—somewhere along the way, I believed that gay people could not be good parents, just because they were gay. It made me sad. I was always close to my sister's kids, but it wasn't enough to be the really devoted uncle; I wanted to be something more for a child. One day I thought, "Why not? Why can't I be a dad?" I could be a great dad for some child. I had a lot of the qualities that make for a great parent.

Some lesbians and gay men with whom I have worked noted that their longing to be parents stemmed from their own positive experiences with family, and the myth that lesbians and gay men could not parent was tinged with sadness, as this man noted here:

I come from a very intact two-parent home, and family has always been the center of our lives, and my parents—being the very good parents that they were—instilled in us the value of family. Family was always very important. When it was clear to me that I was gay, there was a sadness that I could not have children and the coming-out process for me was not about people knowing I was gay, it was more about losing the idea of having children.

Another lesbian mother reconciled the desire to become a parent with living life as an out lesbian:

> I came out when I was 24, but previous to that I always want-
> ed children. I'm one of seven, all my siblings have lots of
> kids, and I just always had in my head that I was going to have
> children. I just always wanted to have children. Then when I
> came out I thought, I guess I'm not having kids. I didn't really
> think twice about it. It didn't cross my mind to get married and
> have children. I thought, I'm not doing that, I'm not living a big
> lie or whatever but that's what it felt like to me when women
> got married to have children and fulfill that parenting desire.
> So I just got totally into my career and then [I got] very active
> in the gay and lesbian community. I never heard of people hav-
> ing children as gays and lesbians; I never heard of that.

Another woman echoed the sentiment of initial sadness about not being able to become a parent and identified the life event that helped her see that she could indeed become a parent.

> Well, it was something that I had always wanted, actual-
> ly. It was probably the only problem I had with being
> gay was that I couldn't be a parent. At least that what I thought.
> But that changed when I was working in Los Angeles and a
> friend was there, a friend from college and she was ill. She
> asked us if her son could stay with us until she got better. Her
> son was just 16 months old. We were so excited, and he stayed
> with us for about nine months. When his mom got better, he
> went back home with her, and at just about the same time…we
> moved to Boston. His leaving left this huge, huge void. So we
> decided to fill that void by trying to adopt a child of our own.

For many lesbians and gay men, meeting another lesbian or gay man who chose to be a parent was a transformative experience in their lives:

> So when my friend Ben, who was an openly gay man, adopt-
> ed his first child and I spent time with him and his partner,
> I realized that I could do it and it opened up a whole new
> world to me.

As with other couples, in some cases, there was one partner who wanted children more than the other:

Definitely Bill felt more strongly. He said that he couldn't live without being a parent and I felt, well, it's not that likely, but if it didn't happen I would try to make something else important and that would be my life. Certainly my nieces and nephews would be more important, as they are to many gay people, kind of like substitute children. But my partner felt like he could not live without them, having children.

Adoption and Fostering

Gay men and lesbians are in a unique position with respect to adoption and fostering (Melina, 1998, p. 296). Most heterosexuals come to the idea of fostering or adoption after trying or considering different ways of creating their own family, such as infertility treatment or donor insemination. Although some lesbians may have infertility issues, tried having sex with a man, or tried donor insemination, for many lesbians and gay men, fostering or adoption is a first choice.

Like all potential adopters and foster parents, lesbians and gay men have had to learn about the process (Brodzinsky, Schechter, & Marantz, 1993). The women and men whom I met were resourceful and gathered information from books (Benkov, 1994; Martin, 1993) and from other people who had adopted or fostered, including heterosexuals, other gay men and lesbians, and agency social workers.

The issue of openness about one's sexual orientation was a clear theme for all of the lesbians and gay men who were considering fostering or adoption. The secondary theme was whether they could adopt:

We wanted so much to become parents and often thought about and talked about adoption. We always kept hearing how many children were in need of homes. I thought that it would be great for a kid who had two parents that loved them. But I wasn't even sure that it was legally possible for gay men to adopt.

Many gay and lesbian prospective parents also are concerned that agencies may offer them the children who have traditionally been the most difficult to place. What strikes psychologist April Martin (1993), author of *The Lesbian and Gay Parenting Handbook*, as ironic is that the same agencies that believe lesbians and gay men are not suitable parents will place with them children who require the most highly skilled parenting. She, and others, have pointed out that nontraditional families have unique strengths that make them excellent, and in some cases, the best homes for certain children. This quotation exemplifies this sentiment:

When I went to the agency to find out more about adoption, they told me that I would have better luck by trying to become a foster parent first. That sounded fine to me, but then they told me that the only children they had for me were children that were born HIV positive. That sounded fine too, I had lots of experience with HIV, I had seen literally hundreds of friends die, but in retrospect, I did not realize at the time that it was a very different disease in children. My son, Julio, was placed with me; he was 18 months old, underweight, sick quite a bit, and required lots of medical treatment. Being a parent to an HIV-positive child has a lot of ups and downs. It requires a style of parenting that most parents never have to deal with. But it was worth every doctor's visit. I am happy to say that today Julio is a healthy 15-year-old, managing and living with HIV.

In addition to understanding the mechanics of the adoption process, it was important also to understand how forming a family by adoption differs from creating a family biologically:

There was so much that we needed to learn about the adoption process, that we always had to keep clearly in our minds that what we were moving toward was going to be a very life-changing event. Biologically, having a baby allowed you prepare for nine months; adopting a child could take nine months, a year, or even more. But more than that, we were talking about a child's life here, not just this intellectual process of being a family. Sometimes that was scary, but also very exciting.

Lesbians and gay men must also decide whether to be open about their sexual orientation. Although foster care agencies approved single men and single women to become foster parents during the 1980s and early 1990s, most lesbians and gay men I met were determined early on, or had been warned by other lesbians or gay men who had become parents, that they should not be open about their sexual orientation. Some still opt for the "don't ask, don't tell" policy. Many gay men and lesbians do choose to be open about their sexual orientation, whereas others identify their partners as "friends" who will help raise the child. Despite the discomfort they felt about "going back in the closet," most took this approach as a matter of expedience, for fear of being rejected as parents. Most resented that they had to do so, but also believed it was the price they had to pay for the gift of becoming a parent.

Most lesbian and gay men who are considering fostering or adoption have probably openly identified as lesbians or gay men for some time (in fact, assessing a potential parent's level of "outness" is critical to the homestudy process), but as coming out is a continual process and not a one-time event, these individuals will as prospective adopters or foster parents experience coming out in ways that are uniquely different in their own families and communities. Becoming parents will inevitability increase their visibility in their communities in different spheres, such as school. This is addressed further in the chapter on assessment.

Dealing With Birthfamily Issues

Social workers will want to explore how the applicant's family of origin has responded to his or her desire to foster or adopt. The lesbians and gay men interviewed had some uncertainty, in general, about whether their families would support their decision to become parents. Although they reported a range of experiences, however, the overwhelming majority said their families had been very supportive. Some families were initially shocked by their child's decision:

> At first my parents were taken aback. They just kept saying, "We don't get it, I thought gay people didn't want to have children." They kept telling me how hard it was going to be and asked if I was sure. After they realized that we had done our homework and had given this parenting thing a great deal of thought, they were very supportive, and have been great grandparents to Tanya. I have been very fortunate I have a very loving family.

Some recalled how their parents seemed to feel the need to warn them about the realities of parenting:

> When I told my father, after we had everything in process, that we were going to adopt, he first said, "Are you sure this is what you want to do?" When I told him yes, he said, well then, great, but be prepared to give up a lot of things that you used to do for yourself. Your focus now will have to be those children.

One man recalled this heart-warming welcoming ceremony from his family for his new son:

> My family was ecstatic when Josh came. I went down that next weekend and, unbeknownst to me, my entire family had assembled. They all showed up—all at one time, every

single one of them. It was unprecedented—this only happened when we had weddings or funerals. I had no idea they were all gathering. When I got there, they all ran out of the house, and my sister grabbed Josh and he didn't know this woman—he was being passed from one person to another. It was a very nice thing; we had a lovely dinner and it was great.

In contrast, one of the women met with complete rejection of her decision to parent by her own parents:

M y family has always been so nonsupportive of my life as a gay person, so it was no surprise when they were completely rejecting of my decision to parent. I told them I planned to adopt and they just rolled their eyes and said, "Do you really think that is fair to those children?" I have dealt with the pain I feel about their rejection of me, but in some small part of my heart, I wished they could have gotten over it and been there for my children as grandparents. I think I have reconciled this pain by realizing that my family is missing so much by not being a part of Joe and Jeremy's lives…they are such beautiful kids.

Whether it was assumed that parents would be supportive or not, a number of the men and women reported that they did not seek the input of their families:

W e didn't tell family, not until it came time; we discussed it a little bit with siblings beforehand, but not parents. I felt like I was over 30, 30 years old, and I felt like this was my personal decision and they only needed to know when it happened. It was not something I really cared for any input on from people. It was between my partner and me, and other people didn't matter, except to be informed. I didn't feel like I needed approval from anyone. It was our decision. When we did tell our families, my family was fine, but my partner's family, especially his father, were very disapproving—so much so that they didn't meet our child until he was 6 months old. That was hard.

Most reported that their parents approved of their decision to become parents. Many were excited by the prospect of having a grandchild (one of the first laments from parents when their son or daughter comes out to them is, "But I wanted grandchildren!"). Their new role of parent often brought gay men and lesbians closer to their own parents. They found new appreciation and sensitivity for their parents' struggles to raise them, and they could rely on the support and guidance of their parents in raising their children. The narratives suggest that no matter how different their parenting style was from their own parents', or how different the circumstances by which they became parents, lesbians and gay men's empathy for their parents increased when they stepped into the role of parent.

Social workers need to be aware of the strong anti–lesbian and gay sentiment held by many religious groups and the effect that this can have on family members for whom sexual orientation is an issue. Families, particularly families with strong religious convictions, may openly condemn homosexuality, unaware that one of their own family members is lesbian or gay (Helminiak, 1997; Herman, 1997). Religious views on gay and lesbian identity vary widely. According to many religious creeds and denominations, sexual relations between people who are not of the opposite sex are forbidden and regarded as sinful, and many religious teaching texts have been erroneously used as a weapon against lesbians and gay men, causing a great deal of distress in many families of faith. Several excellent resources, however, provide an alternative perspective (Cooper, 1994; Metropolitan Community Church, 1990; Parents & Friends of Lesbians and Gays, 1997).

CHAPTER 6

RECRUITING LESBIAN AND GAY ADOPTERS AND FOSTER PARENTS

RECRUITING SUFFICIENT NUMBERS OF FOSTER PARENTS with requisite skills and characteristics is an ongoing challenge for all states (Adopt US Kids, 2004; Groninger, 1992; Meltsner, 1987a, 1987b; Smith & Gutheil, 1988). Ongoing concern about the pool of foster parents inevitably puts the focus on the recruitment and retention of parents.

A report from the Office of the Inspector General (2002a) made several important findings that have relevance for recruiting lesbian and gay men as foster and adoptive parents:

1. *Recruitment efforts do not focus on families willing and able to care for the most challenging children.* Although most foster care agencies use recruiting methods designed to cast a wide net and recruit a large volume of prospective foster parents, many families recruited in this manner are unwilling to care for school-age children, teenagers, and children with special needs. These children constitute the largest portion of children in foster care, thus creating an urgent need to recruit families who are willing and able to provide them with care. Lesbian and gay foster and adoptive families have often proved their willingness to care for the most challenging children (Anderson, Ryan, Taylor-Brown, & White-Gray, 1999).

2. *States are underutilizing their most effective recruitment tool—other licensed foster parents.* Very few states use foster parents regularly in their recruitment efforts, although data suggest that current licensed foster parents are one of the most successful recruitment tools. Foster parents are effective recruiters

because they share information about the need for foster parents through word-of-mouth contact and can promote the idea of fostering just by their presence in the community. Lesbian and gay foster parents and adoptive parents have a strong national network of support; these parents could be very useful in assisting states to recruit other lesbian and gay foster and adoptive families.

3. *Poor public perceptions of foster care and cumbersome requirements have proven to be a deterrent to recruitment.* Poor public perceptions of foster care discourage prospective foster parents. Unfavorable media portrayals depicting tragedies and abuse endured by foster children perpetuate negative perceptions about the current foster care system. Delayed responses to inquiries, stringent requirements, and the length of time involved in becoming a foster parent also adversely affect states' recruitment efforts and reinforce existing reservations about fostering. Most lesbians and gay men who are interested in fostering or adoption have done their homework, are knowledgeable about the licensing and homestudy requirements, and are highly motivated to parent once they have made their decision to do so.

In a study for Casey Family Programs and the National Resource Center for Foster Care and Permanency Planning, Lutz (2002) noted that the first component of a recruitment campaign is the delivery of a clear message that foster parents are valued members of a children's services team.

One can categorize efforts at recruiting new lesbian and gay foster or adoptive families in the same way Barbell and Sheikh (2000) categorized foster parent recruitment for the general population:

- general recruitment, which uses general messages such as "help a child" or "change a life";
- child-specific recruitment, which may be aimed at relatives or other individuals who already know a child, or by using the media to describe a specific child; and
- targeted recruitment, which "focuses on the specific groups of children and teens in need of families and tries to match them with the pool of available families" or on "specific skills needed to meet the needs of certain children" (p. 22).

As a study on the length of time that foster parents serve suggested (U.S. General Accounting Office, 2002), the field has a real crisis in not having enough good-quality foster parents. The types of people who are able to manage these children's needs are going to be extraordinary people, so agencies need to look at every individual who has the capacity to do this. Another study (Evan B. Donaldson, 2003) suggested that a minority of adoption and fostering agencies would refuse to assess lesbians or gay men, but the ways people fail to get through the process are likely to be more subtle and insidious.

With a growing number of children and young people awaiting placement in temporary foster care settings or permanent adoptive settings, agencies may now be more open to considering individuals and couples who they may have traditionally overlooked as prospective foster parents and adopters. Lesbians and gay men, in particular, are being looked to as valuable resources because they bring individual and collective strengths to the adoption and fostering task. Without preconceived notions of what constitutes family, many lesbians and gay men are receptive to adopting or fostering older children, sibling groups, and children with special needs. Many have also experienced adversity in their own lives and as such bring strengths to children and youth who themselves face challenges.

What Works in Recruitment?

Sellick and Thoburn concluded in 1996 that "research into effective approaches [to] recruitment is scarce though some studies and descriptive accounts of practice provide some helpful leads" (p. 112). These studies highlight that agencies need to value parents, and recruitment messages that emphasize characteristics of parents in terms of a person specification may be more likely to attract people to apply, particularly those who may question their own suitability. In addition, Sellick and Thoburn concluded that "informing people about the wider package of training, financial remuneration, post placement support and possibilities of career development is therefore essential" (p. 46).

Word of Mouth

Triseliotis, Shireman, and Hundleby's study (1999) demonstrated that more than half of the current parents interviewed said that they had learned about fostering through relatives and friends or through their work, especially social care jobs. The authors concluded "from the comments we had, it became obvious that the experience of past and current parents are crucial in shaping a public image of fostering" (p. 55). The Office of the Inspector General's (2002a) report focusing on foster care recruitment reinforced the importance of word of mouth as a means of attracting new foster parents.

Many lesbian and gay parents approach agencies after hearing about experiences of fostering and adoption from others in their network. From interviews with current parents, it is evident that experiences of discrimination, rejection, or indifference from agencies become well known in the community, and some agencies have a reputation for not respecting or valuing potential lesbian and gay applicants. It is therefore important for agencies and workers to acknowledge this—most important, staff members need to be comfortable working with lesbians and gay men. This includes all levels of staff, from reception to senior management.

Some states have found that having a presence at community events, such as lesbian and gay pride events or a lesbian and gay expo, works well in attracting interest in fostering and adoption—and taking recruitment actively into the community serves to affirm that the state values and is interested in the community. States have learned similar lessons in the effective recruitment of African American, Latino, and Asian parents.

Use of the Press

Adopt US Kids (2004) and others (Groninger, 1992; Meltsner, 1987a, 1987b) have noted that most recruited foster parents came to know about fostering either through reading a feature article or seeing an advertisement in the press, mostly in their local newspaper. Others (Barbell & Sheikh, 2000; Lutz, 2002) have concluded that television and sometimes local radio have a significant effect on recruitment. Poster displays, leaflets, and staff seemed to have less effect, although they sometimes triggered the final decision to move to action.

Some agencies have made effective use of advertising in the lesbian and gay press (*The Advocate, The Blade*). Advertisements that include images of lesbian and gay couples with children are particularly useful as a means to recruit families. Efforts to recruit African American, Latino, and Asian lesbian and gay adopters and foster parents could be made through advertising in African American, Spanish-language, and Asian community newsletters and publications.

Many have also recognized the importance of specific advertising for lesbian and gay parents in mainstream newspapers and magazines to target people who are not specifically engaged with the lesbian and gay community and may not buy lesbian and gay magazines. Those agencies that have used these forums have found that advertising in the lesbian and gay press attracted white, mainly middle-class parents, and they have used the mainstream press to widen their pool of parents from different backgrounds and ethnic groups.

Current parents that I interviewed have spoken about the effect of seeing advertising that specifically mentioned being lesbian and gay as part of an agency's eligibility criteria—such as on buses and billboards—and felt more confident about approaching these agencies. As one gay parent commented:

W hen I saw that ad, it said to me that they must have given some thought to us being parents; it also signaled to me that I would be welcome to apply and that we might be valued and given a positive response to foster parenting. If they have been more vague, I might not have gotten that message. In the same way, when I recently saw an ad on TV in a western state for foster parenting, they used the words, "Single and married may apply." That very word, "married," signaled to me that they weren't talking about me.

Many agencies do not use the terms *lesbian* or *gay* in their eligibility criteria; they may use phrases such as "in a stable relationship," or "irrespective of sexuality"—but these terms can be unclear or misleading. Use of the terms *lesbian* and *gay*, however, sends a powerful and welcome message to those who might want to be considered as adopters or foster parents. In some cases, states might intentionally want to be subtle; in others, where there are greater legal protections, the direct approach might be warranted.

Initial Inquiry to Agency

The way staff greet applicants when they first make contact with an agency is remembered by many of the interviewees and appears to have an important effect on setting the tone for future contacts. It is clear that a less than warm initial response to a phone call or in the course of an initial interview may well discourage some potentially successful adoptive or foster parents. Those who are finally approved describe how they had to be determined and persistent, and some commented that they fear some potentially good applicants may not survive what they see as an obstacle course designed to keep them out.

This reflects the experience of many lesbian and gay parents when they initially made contact with an agency. Some faced outright rejection and hostility; for others the experience was more subtle, such as being asked early on in the phone call, "What is your husband's/wife's name?" One lesbian foster parent recalled having to deal with a social worker's embarrassment and confusion when she realized she was taking an inquiry from a lesbian couple:

I f she couldn't deal with that, what did it say about the agency and how they would treat us? Clearly, they had not given any thought to the fact that lesbian and gay couples might apply. It also meant I had to come out in response—it did not feel positive, welcoming, or comfortable. (Mallon & Betts, 2005).

In an interview, a lesbian adoptive couple recounted their experience with one state on their first contact. They had asked about the state's previous approvals of gay and lesbian couples, and the staff member told them that the agency had "recently placed a child with a gay couple; he was a child that was so handicapped that he would never know that they were lesbian." Needless to say, this couple did not make an application to that agency.

As suggested by the information provided by Adopt US Kids (2004) to statewide recruitment response teams, responses to initial inquiries need to be friendly, immediate, and in the language of the caller. If specific advertisements or TV spots have been placed, agencies need to be prepared to manage the response to advertising in a positive and efficient manner.

Information Packs

Written information needs to provide clear information regarding eligibility, the task of caring, the characteristics of competent parents, and the needs of children and youth waiting for placement. It may also be useful to include reading material and resources that include references to lesbian and gay adoption and fostering.

Some information packs include examples of different types of families who could foster or adopt, including lesbian and gay families. Vignettes in training may also be useful—several can be found in Appendix A.

Specific Recruitment of Lesbian and Gay Parents

The following questions are important for agencies and professionals to consider when seeking to recruit lesbians and gay men as foster parents and adopters:

- Is the agency's senior management supportive of specifically recruiting lesbian and gay parents? If not, how can the agency address this?

- What training is available to social workers, managers, and panel members in relation to lesbian and gay fostering and adoption? Where can staff access such training?

- Are gay and lesbian families visible anywhere in the agency publications? Are pictures of gay and lesbian families (including African American, Latino, and Asian gay and lesbian families) featured along with other families in agency materials or in photographs displayed throughout the premises?

- Does the agency have a welcoming statement to all families? Is it inclusive of lesbian and gay applicants? Do forms say "applicant" or "foster parent," or do they ask for "male and female" applicants or "husband and wife?"

- Is training inclusive? Are lesbians and gay men depicted in case studies, in examples given, or in training panels?
- What support services is the agency able to offer families? Are other gay and lesbian parents available as mentors? Does the agency offer a support group for lesbian and gay parents? Are staff familiar with resources for lesbian and gay families?

Preparing for Negative Feedback

Negative responses from some politicians, church leaders, and the media have made some states and adoption agencies reluctant to publicize their willingness to recruit lesbians and gay men. The word *lifestyle*, which agencies should avoid in recruitment materials, is often seen as a buzzword for the radical right (Shorteo, 2005). At a time when states face a shortage of people willing and able to take on the complex needs of children in public care, individual workers and managers need to be prepared for negative comments and develop confidence in challenging the myths and stereotypes associated with lesbian and gay parenting.

Conclusions

- Word of mouth is the most effective tool in recruitment, so agencies need to be aware of how lesbian and gay applicants perceive them.
- Use the lesbian and gay press in recruitment drives.
- It is important to use the mainstream press, specifically using the terms *lesbian, gay,* and *partner* rather than the word *marriage* in eligibility criteria and advertising.
- Information packs should include images of lesbian and gay parents and information about lesbian and gay adoption and fostering, such as relevant books and websites.
- Initial contacts are very important. The agency's response should be welcoming and interested. Assumptions should not be made about applicant's partners or family composition.
- Follow-ups to inquiries should be immediate and friendly.
- Senior management in the agency must be supportive of recruiting and supporting lesbian and gay parents.
- Training and support should be available to managers, practitioners, and panels.

CHAPTER 7

Assessment of Lesbian and Gay Foster Parents and Adopters

Deciding to adopt or become a foster parent for a child is a huge step. Potential parents are understandably apprehensive about what the process entails—lesbians and gay men, given their history, may have even greater cause for concern. Overall, large numbers of lesbians and gay men have successfully fostered or adopted, but the view that lesbians and gay men will simply be rejected is still a commonly held perception.

It is well established that most professionals who provide health and social services to foster care and adopted children and their families are heterosexual (Mallon, 2000). During the past decade, agencies have made various efforts to enhance the ability of such professionals to respond effectively to the needs of people who are not heterosexual (Mallon,1999a, 1999b; Mallon & Betts, 2005). These efforts have been largely sporadic, with an emphasis on raising awareness and sensitivity. Additional efforts have sought to increase knowledge and understanding about the history and culture of specific groups of lesbian and gay men. These attempts, however, have not addressed the issue of effective practice in a comprehensive and sustained manner, and although a good beginning, they are less than adequate. "Competent practice with diverse populations" (which has heretofore excluded issues pertaining to sexual orientation from its discussions) has become a phrase in dire need of clarification if we are to move beyond the splintered approaches that have characterized previous efforts.

The Challenge for Professionals

States have a clear imperative to provide effective services for prospective lesbian and gay adopters and foster parents. Social work educators, as well as practitioners, often assume that competence with gay and lesbian groups can be achieved through short-term, and often "one-shot," workshops or gay and lesbian guest speakers in lectures (Mallon, 1997). These assumptions reflect a short-sighted, simplistic view of a complex process. Restructuring one's views and developing a sound base of knowledge and skills should be long-term professional endeavors (Diller, 1999, p. 25).

As in all professional development, no ideal completion point exists. Mallon (1997) described a counselor skilled in issues of sexual orientation as:

> A professional who begins with a well-developed sense of self-knowledge and then expands beyond his or her narrow world views to broadly include a diverse group of persons, including those diversities which pertain to issues of sexual orientation. (p. 222)

Thus, any serious initiative to work effectively with gay and lesbian populations begins with this premise.

As firmly expressed by others (Appleby & Anastas, 1998; Morrow & Messinger, 2006), agencies must pursue preparation for serving gay and lesbian populations effectively on a multidimensional front. A unimodal focus on raising awareness or sensitivity is required but is inadequate by itself. It is unacceptable to believe that increasing one's level of cognitive understanding of lesbians and gay men is all one needs to do. Nowhere is this issue more relevant than during the assessment process.

The Assessment Process

The assessment processes for lesbian and gay male parents or adopters can become skewed if the assessing worker is either overfocusing on sexuality or totally ignoring it. Workers cannot ignore sexual orientation in the assessment process, because an individual's sexuality is an aspect of who they are as a total person and will affect their life as a parent. What needs to be established early on in the assessment is the applicant's ability to constructively manage homophobia and heterocentrism in his or her own life.

The field has moved from the model that has treated gay and lesbian applicants as being the same as their heterosexual counterparts to acknowledging the different experiences that being a gay or lesbian parent brings to fostering and adoption. As gay and lesbian parents have demonstrated their unique strengths as foster parents and adopters, they have had less need to argue that they are "just as good" as heterosexual parents, with the underlying presumption that the heterosexual model of family life is best.

Agencies are required by law to carry out a full assessment of applicants before approving them as foster or adoptive parents. The information to be collected and required checks are detailed in the relevant state regulations and standards. Although this process may vary from state to state, agencies should make prospective parents aware of the flow of this process at the start of their initial engagement with the agency. The Texas Adoption Resource Exchange provides an excellent overview on its website about the steps to becoming a foster or adoptive parent (see http://www.dfps.state.tx.us/Adoption_and_Foster_Care/How_to_Start/steps.asp). This site might be useful for potential foster and adoptive parents to review.

The Concept of Competence

As in any assessment, the values and opinions of the assessor can influence both the process and the outcome of the assessment. Therefore, those doing the assessment need to ensure that they are working with an agreed-on set of values that will specify the spirit in which the assessment should be done. These values should include:

- promoting equality,
- working in a way that challenges discrimination, and
- maintaining confidentiality.

The First Contact

In initial interviews with the individual or couple, social workers must be clear in their language, in their affect, and in setting the tone that they are open to and accepting of lesbians and gay men as parents. Social workers must also be aware that the applicant, at this initial interview, may not be "out." Many lesbian and gay applicants will be assessing both the social worker and the agency for "safety," trying to determine whether the agency will support them. Trust will develop over time, although some lesbians and gay men will come out directly at this first interview.

Jane and her partner, Rebecca, made the following observations about approaching an agency and preparing for a first visit:

> I found myself with a dilemma. So far, I'd yet to phone an agency and ask direct questions about their policies in considering a lesbian couple for adoptive parents. Now I wasn't sure if I'd asked the right questions, or been thorough enough to ensure that the agency we appeared to have chosen (or, actually,

appeared to have chosen us) would have a thorough understanding of lesbian and gay issues in their assessment of us. On
the other hand, there was an equal opportunities statement,
and I knew through contacts that we wouldn't have been the
first gay couple to be considered. I equally didn't want to draw
attention to my sexuality, and highlight it as an issue—when I
didn't think it should be.

I sought advice from online forums (Families Like Mine
and Family Pride Coalition), and tried a new approach—our
state-based adoption resource exchange. As it wasn't a venue
specifically aimed at gay parents, I wasn't sure what kind of a
response I would get, but it was more than just positive. It was
helpful and informative, coming from people who had already
been through the system, and were glad to be realistic, but positive in their assessment of their experience, and in offering
advice. They reassured me that I wasn't going to spend my
entire assessment period justifying my relationship or suitability to parent children.

To our surprise, the social worker who turned up to talk to us about adoption was himself gay. Any doubts we had quickly disappeared, and left us feeling
able to ask questions related to gay issues without feeling we were making an
issue out of being gay. My own concerns related to the potentially homophobic
attitude I may experience from birthparents, rather than from anyone involved in
the assessment process itself, and these fears were answered, and honest consideration given to my "what if" scenarios. Our only other concern was whether we
would be allowed as a gay couple to adopt jointly—but it looks like this won't be
a problem for us because we live in a state where this is possible.

Training Groups

Many lesbian and gay parents say they felt isolated and vulnerable in a MAPP
(Model Approaches to Positive Parenting) or PRIDE (Parent Resource for
Information, Development, Education) training group, and some parents who
were interviewed in the preparation of this book were nervous about dealing with
other group members' homophobia in the group setting. All the parents interviewed recalled that they had not been prepared by their assessing social worker
for the group training, either in general or specifically in relation to their needs
as lesbian or gay parents. Some parents observed that they felt that the onus was

on them to come out at the start of the group. Joyce and Anna commented that both social workers and other group facilitators "did not have a great understanding of what it meant to come out."

In truth, it is likely that there will be a range of reactions in the group—from people who are shocked that states allow lesbians and gay men to adopt or foster to those who are comfortable with and accepting of lesbians and gay men as parents. It is not the prospective parents' responsibility to either manage homophobia from group members or to educate the group; the responsibility for this rests with the facilitating social workers. In this respect, it is important that the trainer sets clear ground rules for the group that refer to accepting and valuing diversity and challenging discriminatory comments.

The Homestudy

Should the homestudy be different for lesbian and gay parents? In her article "Gender, Sex, and Sexuality in the Assessment of Prospective Parents," Helen Cosis-Brown (1992) argued that these areas are an important part of the assessment process, as:

> They are an integral part of our lives and how we see ourselves and are perceived by others, but they are also highly privatized areas and sometimes split off from the rest of our lives. For social workers, addressing this issue in their work can feel like crossing an inappropriate boundary. (p. 32)

In terms of gender, Cosis-Brown (1992) observed that "how people organize themselves, and experience their gender and gender relationships, will have implications for the children placed with them" (p. 30). She argued that "open" family systems are more likely to offer successful placements. "If a couple are being assessed they need to feel comfortable with the roles they have within their household, and have the capacity to negotiate change if and when that is required" (p. 31). With regard to sex and sexuality:

> How we feel about ourselves physically and sexually is likely to have profound implications for the development of children in our care...assessing social workers should be assured that prospective parents have a clear enough sense of their own sexuality and sexual boundaries to help children with their difficult emotional experiences, which may manifest themselves in quite problematic ways. (pp. 32–33)

In his article "Good Lesbian, Bad Lesbian...Regulating Heterosexuality in Fostering and Adoption Assessments", Stephen Hicks (2000) observed that:

> The social work assessment of fostering and adoption applicants rests upon a conflation of "sex—gender—sexuality" so that each is assumed to flow naturally from the other for heterosexual applicants. More importantly the terms are frequently confused within social work assessments, with the result that ideas resting on assumptions about gender (who can do certain caring tasks for example) are linked to those based upon sex (women can do certain tasks and men can do others). (p. 159)

If workers are assessing lesbians, Hicks believes that:

> Anxieties about gender and heterosexuality are raised because the lesbian is regarded as someone who does not fit into the "sex—gender—sexuality" system, her gender roles may be viewed as suspect, she may be seen to influence adversely the gender or sexuality of children, and her lesbianism is always "different" from the usual heterosexuality. (p. 166)

It is important, therefore, to consider how assessing social workers may theorize sexuality. For some, anxieties are raised in relation to the motivation of lesbians and gay men, their capacity to parent, and their gender roles.

As lesbian and gay people seek to raise children in growing numbers, social workers increasingly have the opportunity to do homestudies for these families. The training these workers receive in lesbian and gay issues and doing homestudies for these families varies, and expectations and standards continually change. What is accepted practice in an urban area with large numbers of gay and lesbian applicants may be unheard of in a more rural area where workers have less lesbian and gay adoption and fostering experience.

Lesbian and gay adoption and foster care is changing quickly and dramatically across the United States. Because of the enormous variation in policies, expectations, practices, and cultures across the United States, it may be impossible to agree on one best nontraditional homestudy format. Homestudy formats vary from state to state, but recent changes in the some state laws move the development of these guidelines an important step in the right direction. They:

- give social workers a sense of the formats other agencies are currently using to write homestudies for lesbian and gay applicants, and

- provide general cultural competency information so that those who work with lesbian and gay applicants can do so in a sensitive, respectful manner.

A Continuum of Homestudy Formats

The following sections, adapted from Solot's (1998) work, present several formats that agencies are currently using for homestudies for prospective lesbian and gay adoptive and foster parents. As with heterosexual applicants, the issues can be quite different for single adoptive and foster parents compared with couples. When single people adopt or foster, often their sexual orientation is not known, or it seems less important; the issue of adopting as a single person often becomes the primary one rather than sexual orientation.

Single Lesbians and Gay People: Out or Not?

When a gay or lesbian person does not currently have a partner and wishes to adopt as a single person, the homestudy can be written as any other single applicant. It is not important to always directly ask applicants about their sexual orientation, although the applicant may disclose this information in the process of discussions about his or her past and future.

If the worker does not know how the person identifies after the standard home visits, it is usually acceptable practice to write the homestudy without reference to the subject. The worker describes the person as single, can mention any major past relationships or marriages (sometimes applicants do not mention past partners' genders in their paperwork), and can indicate the applicant's thoughts on relationships in the future.

If the applicant tells the worker he or she is lesbian or gay, the worker may discuss with the applicant how this information should be included in the homestudy. It may be mentioned as descriptive (i.e., "Mary is a single, self-identified lesbian woman living in suburb of Hartford") or in more detail in the applicant's autobiography or description of past and anticipated future relationships. Some applicants feel more comfortable having this information included in the homestudy so that he or she does not have to worry about hiding information from children's workers he or she may meet with in the future. This way, the applicant knows that anyone who approaches him or her with a possible match is aware of the situation.

Other workers and applicants may feel that sexual orientation is not necessary to share and that as a single person, it has no relevance to the applicant's ability to parent a child. Some workers routinely advise gay or lesbian single people that they will not include this information in the homestudy because it is irrelevant. Workers who consider themselves "allies" for lesbian or gay applicants in more conservative agencies or states may decide that not mentioning a single lesbian or gay person's sexual orientation is not only valid, it will remove the barrier of homophobia that could delay or deny appropriate placements.

Same-Gender Couples: As a Two-Parent Family

Increasing numbers of social workers are doing homestudies of gay and lesbian couples the same way they do homestudies of heterosexual couples. Both people's names are listed as the adoptive or foster parents, and both receive an equal amount of attention in the homestudy.

The homestudy is written in the same format as if the couple were male-female, including information about the length of their relationship (because same-gender couples cannot marry, information about marriage would not apply) and its strengths and weaknesses.

Many social workers have said they prefer this type of straightforward homestudy because it gives them a better understanding of the type of family that may be adopting or fostering a child or youth on their caseload, but some states' policies or laws may not allow homestudies to be written in this way.

This format is groundbreaking in some places; it also is a very natural way to write this important document. But most lesbian and gay people are applying to adopt because they want to be parents, not because they want to be groundbreakers.

Same-Gender Couples:
As a Single Parent With a Domestic Partner

A modification on the two-parent homestudy is the single parent with a "domestic partner" homestudy. Some social workers choose this approach because of laws or policies that require same-gender couples to adopt as single people, or because other social workers in their agency or part of the country are more comfortable with this format. The homestudy is written primarily about one partner, focusing on that person's social history and interest in adoption and listing his or her name alone as the adoptive or foster parent. The second partner is included in the homestudy process and is described in the homestudy as a domestic partner or "friend." The homestudy describes the length of their relationship and cohabitation, and it explains that both partners will consider themselves parents of the child to be adopted.

This type of homestudy is clearly a hybrid: It is honest about the situation of the couple, but conforms to current policies about lesbian and gay adoption. In agencies or states in which people are uncomfortable or unwilling to consider a homestudy with two same-gender parents, this approach may be a good fit. It can be, however, confusing to see one person listed as the adoptive or foster parent when a couple is really a two-parent family. The format may misleadingly suggest to children's workers that this family consists of a "primary parent" and the parent's partner, instead of two parents who will share parenting responsibilities.

Same-Gender Couples:
As a Single Person With a Roommate

Until recently, most homestudies of same-gender couples were written using this format. The homestudy describes one partner as a single parent, and the entire homestudy focuses on this person alone. Because homestudies are required to list other individuals in the home, the other partner is listed as a roommate, and the agency obtains criminal clearances for him or her. Very little other information about the relationship is mentioned, although often a sentence is included saying that this person is supportive of the "roommate's" plans to adopt.

This type of homestudy can be the safest in a state or agency that is extremely uncomfortable with gay and lesbian adoptions, or it may be mandated by policy or law. This type can be problematic if is not clear to a person reading this type of homestudy what this family's structure really is. Some social workers reading the homestudy may take it at face value, assuming this is truly a single-parent family. Other social workers may read between the lines and wonder what the relationship is between the two "roommates." When a child's worker expresses interest in placing a child with the "single parent," he or she may be given more information about the situation verbally or in writing.

Although this approach to writing a gay or lesbian homestudy seemed the safest way to do so when workers created these homestudies in the early 1980s, some families have found that today, this method can backfire. One child's worker thought a specific child on her caseload would do extremely well placed with a single man and selected a single-person homestudy written in this way. After investing considerable time pursuing the match, she found out that it was actually a two-parent family, not the situation she believed could best meet this child's needs (although she had positive experiences placing other children with gay or lesbian couples in the past). She also raised concerns that if the agency—not one with which she had worked previously—was willing to omit such major information about the family from the homestudy, she felt less willing to trust that other important information had not been omitted. Social workers and agencies that choose to follow this format should do so with these concerns in mind.

Workers should always write homestudies with the best interest of the child or youth in mind, not the best interest of the potential parent. It is important to heed the words of adoption expert Joyce Maguire Pavao (2005), who reminds us that adoption is about finding families for children, not about finding children for families.

Issues to Address in a Homestudy

Many issues are common to all homestudies, regardless of the sexual orientation of the prospective parents. Gender, sex, and sexuality are important areas for the worker to consider in all assessments, but for lesbian and gay parents, homestudies should address the following specific areas.

People's Experience of Their Lesbian or Gay Identity, and Their Own and Their Family's Response

Clearly, sexual orientation will be an issue to be fully and openly discussed at this point in the assessment process. Many lesbians and gay men who have been through this process found that some social workers either unnecessarily focused on their sexuality too much, or conversely, did not address the issues of sexuality at all. Cosis-Brown (1991) noted further that lesbian and gay applicants have spent a lot more time thinking about their sexuality than most heterosexuals have and that the reticence to address this issue more often lies with the social worker.

Many prospective applicants write their autobiographies as part of the assessment process, and they may choose to address issues relating to their sexual orientation as part of this. For many lesbians and gay men, realizing their sexual orientation and coming out to friends and family is a significant life event, as is meeting their partner. The autobiography should not focus on issues relating to sexual orientation, because this is only one part of a whole person's life experience. Neither should the applicants be encouraged to hide or downplay this aspect of their lives.

Additional questions could be considered, such as: When did you first feel different in terms of your sexuality? Who did you talk to? Where did you find support?

How Confident Do They Feel in Relation to Their Sexual Orientation? How Comfortable Are They as Lesbians or Gay Men?

It will be important to explore with potential parents their experience of coming out and the effect this process has had on their significant relationships in their family and community. Assessing potential parents' level of outness and exploring with them at what point in their development they actually did come out are an important element of practice, as is understanding the need to hide or selectively disclose one's orientation. Comfort level with one's outness is a key factor for the prospective lesbian and gay adopter or foster parent, as being uncomfortable about being out can complicate the parenting process. Being comfortable with being out suggests that a person has integrated his or her lesbian or gay sexual orientation into his or her life.

Some questions social workers may consider here are:

- At what point did you consider coming out to others?
- Are you out in the community? at work? with your family? with friends?
- Are you out to your partner's parents and extended family?
- What has been the attitude of your extended family to your partner? Have they been inclusive and welcoming?
- Is your family supportive of you (and your partner) fostering or adopting a child?

Some lesbians and gay men and their partners are cut off from their extended families because their relatives are unable or unwilling to respect their identity. Of course, applicants should not be penalized because of their extended family's choices, but this information should be included so a worker reading the assessment has a picture of the broader family system the child would join. In addition, a social worker should be available to explore what support networks are available to the potential adopter or foster parent.

Other Issues to Address

Some questions social workers may consider in this area are:

- How have homophobia and heterosexism impinged on the potential parents' lives, how have they dealt with this, and what present coping devices do they use?
- What are their present relationships—sexual, emotional, supportive, family, and so forth? How do they negotiate homophobia in close relationships, such as with their siblings?
- With reference to the future, have they thought about relating to birthparents? What about relationships with other parents, such as at school, in a playgroup, and so forth? How much research

have they done in relation to attitudes of local institutions, such as schools? How would they help a child who experiences prejudice because of his or her parent's sexual orientation?

Partnerships and Relationships

Some debate exists about whether social workers should ask applicants about their sexual relationships, and if they do ask, what should be done with this knowledge? Cosis-Brown (1992) argued that questions about sexual relationships should be part of the assessment for all couples. She stated:

> Firstly, sex is a form of communication…and secondly, sex is a source of pleasure…How we feel about ourselves physically and sexually is likely to have profound implications for the development of children in our care. How children feel about themselves physically and sexually will also have implications for how they relate to others and society. This is all part of developing a good enough sense of self, and helping this development is one of the major tasks for prospective parents. (p. 32)

Parents will meet with challenges in dealing with their adolescents' sexuality, and they have a responsibility to help young people think about the nature of sexuality and relationships and provide them with information about safe sex.

Workers need to explore the following questions relating to significant relationships with *all* applicants:

- What qualities does each partner bring to the relationship?
- What makes the relationship positive for each partner? How do partners support each other? How do they cope with stress and difficulties?
- How will a new child affect this relationship—for example, how will they cope with a child who becomes attached readily to one partner and much more slowly to the other?
- Have the partners considered and explored other options as pathways to parenthood?
- How do they make decisions? Is there wider family involvement in the decisionmaking process?
- What are the strengths and vulnerabilities of the partnership?
- Have there been previous significant relationships, and if so, what has been learned from these? Do they affect the present

partnership? Are there children from any previous relationships, and if so, how will those children be affected by the decision to become parents?

Other Adult Members of the Household

This includes significant adults who live with applicants as well as those who do not. What is their relationship to the applicants? What is their attitude to the proposed placement, and how important is that attitude to the applicants? Issues of sexual orientation may be relevant here.

Motivation

For lesbians and gay men, questions relating to motivation are very relevant for discussion because creating families by birth may not have been an option. Fostering and adoption is often their first choice.

Integration of One's Lesbian or Gay Identity

For lesbian and gay prospective adopter or foster parents, an experienced and competent worker should inquire about the prospective parents' life, but should not overemphasize the lesbian or gay issues. In reality, most lesbians and gay men have a gay or lesbian life, not a gay or lesbian "lifestyle." Being lesbian or gay has become a part of who they are as people, not the entire issue. Some lesbians and gay men attend gay or lesbian venues, such as lesbian and gay community centers, and some do not. Prospective parents may need to evaluate the way individuals or couples spend their recreation and leisure time.

What representations of lesbian or gay relationships do they have in their household, such as pictures and sculptures? In some cases, do these need to change, not because they are gay or lesbian images, but because they might be inappropriate images to have around children?

Valuing Difference

Most lesbians and gay men have experienced discrimination. Most can, therefore, understand the effect on children and youth who have experienced discrimination and being different.

The Child in Placement

How will parents discuss their sexual orientation with the child? How will they support a child in the community and address any homophobic comments the child experiences? How do they view emerging sexuality in adolescence, and how would they ensure an appropriate sexual education? What would they include in this?

One Approach: Anticipate the Concerns

Some social workers have success helping lesbian and gay families adopt or foster by using a strategy in which they attempt to anticipate every concern a child's social worker might have. They first discuss these concerns openly with the prospective adoptive or foster parents and then address each concern openly in the homestudy. This allows the family's worker to use the homestudy to educate, as in:

> Some workers worry that if they place a boy with a gay couple, he will grow up to be gay. However, all the studies that have been done on this subject show that children raised by gay men are no more likely to be homosexual than children raised by heterosexual people.

This approach also allows the family to address potential concerns before they become major barriers. For instance, "Bill and Sam realize that workers may fear that a child placed with them could be teased because he or she has 'two dads.' Here is how they plan to handle this issue if it arises."

Barriers particularly apply to single men adopting because of unfounded stereotypes that they are less stable or want to adopt children to meet their sexual needs. A worker using this "anticipate everything" method may choose to emphasize in a single man's homestudy his healthy adult relationships, the stability of his life, and (if he agrees that it would be beneficial to the goal of adopting a child) how he is getting his sexual needs met. Obviously, any worker using this method must explain the practical theory behind it and decide with the family whether it is a method they feel would be helpful.

Mistakes to Avoid

Keep in mind that sexual orientation and gender identity is only one aspect of who someone is; it should not be a major focus of a homestudy or child placement decisions (Nelson, 1997).

It is not appropriate to address who will parent the child if a same-gender couple splits up, unless this is a standard part of your agency's homestudy for a married male-female couple (this is not commonly a standard part of a homestudy). If your professional assessment is that any couple's relationship—regardless of sexual orientation—is not strong enough to survive the challenges of parenting an adopted child, it is questionable whether that couple should be approved to adopt. If, however, your opinion is that the relationship is strong and stable, writing about a potential breakup inappropriately implies that a same-gender relationship cannot be as strong as a marriage and that it cannot be expected to last.

It is not appropriate to address a prospective parent's sex life, unless this is a standard part of your agency's homestudy for a married male-female couple (this, too, is not commonly a standard part of a homestudy). It is appropriate to discuss applicants' personal experience with sexual abuse, to assess how well the applicants are prepared to parent a child with a history of sexual abuse or sexual acting-out behaviors, and to discuss how they expect to deal with issues of sexuality with an adopted child. These discussions, however, need not be different with lesbian- and gay-headed families than heterosexual families.

It is a mistake to assume that same-gender couples assume roles in their relationship where one plays the man and the other plays the woman. Although this is a popular misconception, it is not the reality for most gay and lesbian couples.

Do not ask about a prospective parent's HIV status unless this is a standard question asked of all applicants.

Do not assume that a child or adolescent whose words or behavior suggest he or she is questioning his or her sexual orientation or gender identity should be placed with a family who can "cure" the child and make him or her heterosexual.

Final Decisionmaking

The responsibility of the social worker, his or her supervisor, and in some cases, an interdisciplinary team is to ensure that the assessor's recommendation is based on information that provides relevant, sufficient evidence of the applicant's ability to meet the requirements for being an adoptive or foster parent. The team must then decide whether to endorse the recommendation.

The values and attitudes of team members are often an issue. Recurring themes from an untrained team with respect to lesbian and gay adopters or parents may include the following homophobic responses:

- "Where is the positive male/female role model?"
- "Who is the mother?"
- "How will you explain your relationship to children placed with you?"
- "Won't you make them gay?"

Kevin and Dom, two dads, spoke of their experience with a decision team:

The supervising social worker who was the chair was very rude. He said the worst insult to a child would be being called queer. He also asked us if we thought that our children would become lesbian or gay. He was clearly ignorant about the reality of lesbian and gay people's lives, but we tried to keep our cool and helped him see that we would be good parents. Other folks on the team were clearly uncomfortable with his homophobic remarks. You feel really vulnerable in these situations; these folks have power over whether or not you will be approved, but it is very unsettling. We should not have to "prove" ourselves worthy, more than any other candidate.

Arthur and Tom, who have had a baby girl placed with them, were asked by their social worker about role models; one of the issues that arose in connection with this was that they would not be able to teach a girl to put on make-up and do her hair. Both men laughed and said they were probably better placed to teach these skills than many women they knew, given that they both were hairstylists. Their social worker also observed that they had identified an extensive list of female relatives and friends in their support networks—and here they did more work than would have been expected by heterosexual applicants.

Matching and Placement

Once approved, families can be approved to provide care in four general categories:

- foster care,
- foster or adoptive homes,
- legal-risk homes, and
- adoptive homes.

A number of gay and lesbian parents have found that placing social workers can be very conservative in their notion of what constitutes family. This might limit matching of a child or youth to a family, but training for social workers can really help improve practice in this area and facilitate appropriate matches and at the same time promote thoughtful matching practice.

Conversely at this point, agencies deem some applicants, whether they are lesbian or gay or not, not acceptable as foster or adoptive parents; some may be encouraged to apply again later, others will be urged to reconsider their reasons for wanting to parent. When prospective parents are not dealt with in a full and open disclosure style of practice, at this point in the process, social workers may feel vulnerable about being accused of being biased against a lesbian or gay prospective parent. Social workers who do feel uncomfortable discussing nonapprovals need to work with their supervisors and attend specialized training sessions designed to assist them in developing skills in how to discuss how one deals with prospective foster or adoptive candidates who are not approved. The PRIDE training curriculum offers some advice to social workers dealing with these sensitive issues.

Also at this juncture, the child's birthparents or previous foster parents may also object to the placement on the basis of sexual orientation. As Hicks and McDermott (1999) acknowledged:

> All foster parents have to deal with difficult reactions from birth parents looking for reasons to object to the placement of their child. Lesbian and gay foster parents are particularly vulnerable to such objections because of their marginal and contested position in relation to childcare and it is important that agencies which use lesbian and gay parents are prepared to demonstrate full confidence in their parents and support them against homophobic reactions. (p. 172)

The same issues are present in adoption.

The other critical issue is the preparation of children or youth who will be matched with the lesbian or gay parent. Preparation could take the form of a book prepared by the adopter on his or her family that social workers can share with the children. Publications written by the children of lesbian and gay parents (Garner, 2004; Howey, Samuels, Cammermeyer, & Savage, 2000; Snow, 2004) may also be useful tools to assist workers in preparing youth for placement with a lesbian or gay parent. Ryan's (2000) work examining social workers' placement recommendations of children with gay and lesbian adoptive parents may also provide useful guidance for workers. When he or she provides adequate preparation, the worker facilitates an opening for the discussion about the adopters being lesbian or gay. Workers need to develop a set of skills that will assist them in fully discussing the range of issues that may come up and demonstrate a willingness, with full and open disclosure, to exploring and processing these issues together. A range of initial responses may occur; some young people may be surprised that their new home will have lesbian or gay parents, whereas others may have little or no reaction. Regardless of gender or sexual orientation issues, all children and youth who are in foster care or adoptive situations need preparation for living with a new family. The parents I have spoken with recalled that few of their children were well prepared for placement, let alone with a different sort of family. Tom and Peter observed:

> The preparation of our two boys for placement in our family was nonexistent. Little was said to the boys directly; their initial questions to us showed a lack of preparation—they asked "Are you brothers?" They had no concept of what *gay* meant. The boys were also confused about what to call us. We worked it out, but it would have been so much better for the boys if they had transitioned into our home with the knowledge that their family now consisted of two dads who were gay and if someone had talked with them about what that meant.

One social worker I met recalled that following a placement of a child with a lesbian couple, it became clear that the social worker had a homophobic attitude and found it difficult to manage the meeting and talk with the couple. Sessions were rushed and hurried, and when the couple queried when they could complete their adoption application, he stated, "When I say so." This statement was clearly an inappropriate response. This couple now has a lesbian social worker who is out, so the couple does feel more supported.

More resources are increasingly available to help applicants and social workers address these issues.

Conclusions

- Applicants need information about preparation groups, including help identifying any potential areas of difficulty.
- A homestudy assessment gives a framework for assessing applicants' potential as parents of foster or adoptive children and youth.
- When undertaking the assessment, it is important that social workers address specific issues related to sexuality.
- Team members should have access to appropriate training and advice.
- Children and youth need to be prepared for placement with families who are not their birth family.

- Practitioners must be confident and prepared to challenge hete-rocentric assumptions and comments from supervisors, placing social workers, birthfamily members, and in some cases the team when considering placements with lesbian and gay parents.

CHAPTER 8

SUPPORTING LESBIAN AND GAY FOSTER PARENTS AND ADOPTERS

LIKE OTHER FOSTER PARENTS AND ADOPTERS, gay men and lesbians are interested in seeking ways to incorporate their children into their lives and help them make a smooth transition into family life. Like their heterosexual counterparts who adopt or become foster parents, they will at various times need support to sustain and maintain these connections. They also want to meet other lesbians and gay men who have taken on the challenge of parenting.

Many children and young people who are fostered or adopted will have experienced trauma, abuse, or disruption of prior placements. Given their experiences, they are likely to present challenging and difficult behavior. Quinton, Rushton, Dance, and Mayes (1998), in their study of children joining new families, noted that the rate of clinical disorders among these children was almost five times greater than in the general child population and approximately twice that found among groups of children and youth in foster care. Such results indicate the severity of the issues that adoptive parents may encounter. Parents in the Quinton et al. study most frequently expressed the need for support with respect to managing and controlling children's disruptive behavior.

Children's challenging behavior also has consequences outside the home, such as with the extended family, community, and school. Quinton, Rushton, Dance, and Mayes (1998) highlighted the substantial problems of children's relationships with other children, in particular because of their inability to pay attention when playing games, poor understanding of the rules, overenthusiasm in interactions, insensitivity to the feelings of other children, quarrelling, and aggressive behavior.

Parents in this study identified the need for support in managing relationships with a child's birthfamily, which can be complicated, unfamiliar, and stressful. These newly created families need postpermanency services to help them stay together and manage issues as they arise.

An Office of the Inspector General (2002b) report that focused on foster care retention made some important findings about supporting these valuable resources:

- Foster families reported that they desired greater opportunity to voice their concerns.
- Foster parents expressed difficulty establishing positive rapport with caseworkers.
- Foster parents are finding it increasingly difficult to obtain necessary support services, such as respite, child care, and dental, medical, and mental health care for the children in their care.
- Foster parents found it difficult to deal with allegations of abuse by foster children.

Clearly, foster parents and adoptive parents are in need of support, empathy, and guidance as they go about caring for their families.

Informal Support

Informal networks are important in the provision of support for parents, but these may change as a result of placement changes. Some parents pointed out that once they had embarked on adoption, their existing informal support began to diminish, particularly if some people disapproved of what they were doing or found a child's behavior unacceptable. Families change when children are introduced into them, therefore, many lesbians and gay parents interviewed noted how their relationships with single lesbians or gay men changed once children entered their lives. Children coming into placement are also likely to be confronted with the need to establish new sources of informal support.

Specific Postplacement Support Issues for Lesbian and Gay Adopters and Parents

As with other parents, lesbian and gay adopters and parents should have access to postplacement support; however, agencies need to take particular factors into account to provide effective support for lesbian and gay adopters and parents.

In April 2004, the British group Family Futures Consortium held a one-day workshop for gay and lesbian foster and adoptive parents. One of the conclusions from the day was the following:

> The journey to parenthood for all parents is often complex and challenging. It is our experience that it is more so for gay and lesbian parents. Despite the liberalization of legislation and professional practice in the field of social work, the reality is that gay and lesbian parents' parent in a homophobic world and risk rejection by family, friends and wider society. For this reason Family Futures believes that it is very important that there is a clear identification and definition of the particular experience and needs of this group of parents in order that the service-providing professional world is more aware and more empathetic. The function of this workshop was to provide a starting point and forum for these issues to be addressed. The workshop was intended to provide a meeting place for parents where their personal experience of parenthood could be shared and reviewed in the context of Family Futures experience of offering attachment focused support programme. (Family Futures Consortium, 2004)

Twenty-two parents participated in the day. They identified various issues that have implications for agencies when considering their delivery of effective support to gay and lesbian parents and adopters:

- Loneliness and isolation—overlapping issues of being a lesbian or gay parent with a child who has attachment difficulties.
- Validity as a parent and as a family—as a lesbian or gay parent, how do you present yourself to the world and negotiate the world and the tension this causes?
- Rejection and fear of rejection for themselves as parents or for their children as children of gay parents.
- The perception of lesbian and gay families as second best.
- The issue of secrets and secrecy. One group member said, "Living with gay or lesbian parents often confused the normal message that foster or adoptive parents will give their children of 'we have no secrets.' For the protection of their children, gay and lesbian parents often have to negotiate with their children who they can and can't tell about some facets of family

life...gay and lesbian parents often felt confused, fearful, or in a double bind about the issue of openness and secrecy."

The group acknowledged that:

Experiences of homophobia...might result in lesbian and gay parents deciding not to seek help and or guidance from the very professionals who are employed to serve them. In this instance, the risk of parents becoming increasingly isolated and thereby depleted is of grave concern.

The need for ongoing support and an opportunity to share commonalities and differences in a safe space was felt to be essential for individuals to continue to work through their own issues and to better understand how these influence and affect the unique relationships between parent and child. Although all of the participants acknowledged that things had improved, the effects of homophobia in the personal, public, and professional areas of life "continue to be deeply disturbing."

The group felt that their unique experiences of being lesbian and gay adults could contribute to their overall effectiveness as parents, given their ability to empathize with difference and cope with rejection.

Adoption and fostering professionals supporting gay and lesbian parents need to be aware of these issues and how they might affect parents and children. This book has already highlighted the importance of peer support, and agencies perhaps need to consider how best to facilitate support groups for gay and lesbian parents. There are several national organizations (see Appendix B) that might be able to help. Circles of Support, a collaboration between New York City's Administration for Children's Services and the Lesbian, Gay, Bisexual, and Transgender Community Center in New York City recently received funding from the Administration for Children's Services to work with gay and lesbian foster parents and adopters and has set up a monthly support group as part of this initiative.

Characteristics of Postpermanency and Adoption Support Services

Information and details about the types of comprehensive postplacement and adoption support services that families might require are familiar to adoption and fostering social workers. Freundlich and Wright (2003) and Pavao (2005) covered these comprehensively.

In the context of gay and lesbian adopters and parents, agencies should consider some specific issues. Some of the characteristics of support services for gay and lesbian families are as follows:

- Postplacement and adoption support staff are available and competent to work with lesbian and gay families.

- Staff pull together information from many sources to assess the situation. For example, they retrieve case records, talk with teachers and other professionals, procure specialized assessments when needed, and gather the perspectives of all family members. Staff spend extra time with families to give them a chance to fully discuss the difficulties they have experienced and what attempts they have made to find solutions. At this stage, staff should be truly empathetic listeners so families can share their feelings with minimal interruption. Staff should also be able to identify when the issues in placement are related to the sexual orientation of the parent and when that clearly has no bearing.

- Staff use a range of interventions, including support groups (for adults and for the children or youth in families), meetings, and advocacy for resources.

- It is important that staff help families think about how adoption or fostering has affected their lives and relationships.

- Families need to learn about the effects of trauma and abuse as well as the effect of separation and loss, and have support in managing contact issues. Continued post permanency training is important.

- Staff need to help adopters and foster parents take care of themselves and depersonalize children's behavior. "It's not my fault!" and "My child's behavior is normal in light of her history" are important messages that parents can internalize through good adoption support work.

- Staff must also help adopters and foster parents adapt to the normal developmental changes that occur for their child, such as adolescence. Staff must be comfortable differentiating the adopter or foster parent's sexual orientation issues from the child's developmental issues. One adopter made this astute comment about his son's developmental changes:

I have always taken such a pride in being a "good" parent, maybe I have tried too hard to be a perfect parent. My son always could come to talk to me about anything. Then, when he turned 12, it was like he was a different kid. He ignored me, he was embarrassed to be with me, and he was so bold and nasty. I was devastated. I immediately thought it was because he was getting teased at school for having a gay father. I had these notions that it was all because I was this gay adoptive parent. Finally, one day when I was talking with a straight couple that I am friends with, who have a 14-year-old daughter, they set me straight and told me she behaved in the same way. These people were great parents and I trusted them. I realised at that point, and actually felt kind of stupid about it, that it has less to do with me as a gay parent, and much more to do with my son becoming an adolescent.

Although many foster parents and adoptive parents may be vulnerable to feeling that they have to prove their worthiness as parents, lesbian and gay parents might be particularly vulnerable in different ways than are their heterosexual counterparts. Supportive services that acknowledge the particular vulnerabilities and strengths of lesbian and gay parents and that can help them understand the context of their children's difficulties can contribute to the maintenance of successful placements. Acknowledging the strengths of lesbian and gay parents is also an important aspect of supporting these parents.

Conclusions

- It is important that agencies provide peer support and a safe space to explore issues, such as an online resource like Families Like Ours or, for youth, a support program like COLAGE (Children of Lesbians and Gays Everywhere!; see Appendix C).

- Agencies should know about and provide lesbian and gay applicants with information and link them into support groups.

- Adoption and fostering professionals need to recognize the particular vulnerabilities and strengths of lesbian and gay parents.

- It is important that agencies provide accessible and ongoing postapproval training.

CASE VIGNETTES

Hugo and Jorge

Hugo Perez is a 38-year-old, openly gay man who lives with his partner of 12 years, Jorge Sanchez, age 50. Both men are out as gay in the community, to their birth-families, to their colleagues at work, to everyone. On a scale of 1 to 10, with 10 being totally out and 1 being totally closeted, they both answer that they are a 9. Neither man has ever been married to a woman, and both have financially secure careers as civil service office workers in a government office in Taos, New Mexico. Hugo is of Latino heritage—Venezuelan—and Jorge is Mexican American. Both grew up in New Mexico and both are close to their birthfamilies.

Hugo and Jorge come to your agency for an initial exploratory discussion about adoption and subsequently enroll in PRIDE training. Hugo seems much more eager to parent than does Jorge. Both have been open about their ambivalence toward making a commitment to parenting, but feel if they do not do it now, they never will. They come to every training and both fully participate.

- How does this ambivalence of commitment make you feel?
- Hugo and Jorge clearly have issues to explore; what are they?
- How much does this vignette have to do with the men's sexual orientation?

Paula and Barbara

Paula Parker is a 28-year-old lesbian who lives with her partner of six months, Barbara Simmons, age 48. Both women are out as lesbians in the community, but are not out to their birthfamilies or to their colleagues at work. Neither woman has ever been married to a man, and both have financially secure careers as teachers in a local Des Moines, Iowa, high school. Paula is a well respected 9th-grade English teacher and Barbara is the assistant principal at the school where they both work. Paula is of mixed racial heritage and grew up in Europe, and Barbara is, as she said in her interview, a "typical white Anglo-Saxon Protestant." Barbara grew up in New York City.

Paula, without Barbara, comes to your agency for an initial exploratory discussion about adoption and subsequently enrolls in PRIDE training. Paula seems very authentic; she is intelligent, seems emotionally balanced, and seems ready to make a commitment to parenting. During the training, it becomes clear that she has a live-in roommate and, when probed, acknowledges that it is she and not her "roommate" who desires to become a foster parent.

- How does this lack of disclosure make you feel?
- This couple clearly has issues to explore; what are they?
- How much does this vignette have to do with the women's sexual orientation?

Deb and Charlotte

Deb is a white, self-identified lesbian, age 38. Her partner of 10 years, Charlotte, is 48, Latina, and also self-identified as a lesbian. On a scale of 1 to 10 with 10 being completely out, and 1 being not out at all, both women agree they would probably rate themselves an 8. Before meeting Charlotte, Deb was married to a man for five years and has a 10-year-old son, Tommy, who lives with them. Deb has sole custody of her child and has no relationship with her former husband.

Deb, Charlotte, and Tommy live together in a small, private home, which they own in Baton Rouge, Louisiana. Deb is a stay-at-home mom but works part-time as a waitress on the weekends at a bowling alley, and Charlotte works as a kindergarten teacher for the local public school. She makes about $45,000 per year. Both women have graduated from high school. Charlotte has a bachelor's of arts degree from Louisiana State University.

Deb and Charlotte feel competent as parents, feel secure in their relationship together, and have approached the local parish office to apply to become foster parents or adoptive parents for a child. They are not really sure about the difference between foster care and adoption, and they have had no previous experience with the child welfare system. They are open to providing a home for either a boy or a girl between the ages of 6 and 12 years old.

Both women have supportive families. Deb's mother and two sisters live in Baton Rouge and are very involved in Tommy's life and with Deb and Charlotte. Charlotte was adopted when she was five, she has very few memories of her birthfamily and has not conducted a search for them, her adoptive parents have been deceased for five years, and she has a close relationship with two of her cousins, who live in New Orleans.

Both women are open to attending the required MAPP training and looking forward to starting the foster parenting process.

- What are the issues in this family?
- How do you proceed?

How About It, Jose?

Jose Ramirez is a 44-year-old, never-married Latino man of Mexican heritage who comes to your agency for an initial exploratory discussion about adoption and subsequently enrolls in MAPP training. He states clearly on Day 1 of the training that he has a very strong desire to become a parent to a Latino or mixed-heritage child ages 8 to 13 years old and that he is open to a sibling group of three or more. Jose is a very successful production manager at the New York City Opera, makes more than $330,000 a year, owns his own home in Manhattan, and is an accomplished pianist with an master's of fine arts from Julliard. A native New Yorker, Jose states that he has no desire to relocate and has expressed several times during the training that he has no interest in marrying, saying vaguely that he "tried that already several years ago."

Jose seems very authentic; he has clearly done his homework about the child welfare system and seems ready to make a commitment to parenting. But there is something about Jose that you cannot quite put your finger on. It seems as though he is holding back some information, and the more you get to know him, the less clear it becomes.

- How do you proceed?
- What are the issues in this vignette?
- Do you think sexual orientation is an issue; if so or if not, how do you proceed?

There's Something About Mary

Mary Williams, a 34-year-old, divorced, African American woman, comes to your PRIDE training. She states clearly on Day 1 that she has a very strong desire to become a parent to an African American child ages 8 to 13 years old and is open to a sibling group. Mary is a bank manager in Kansas City, Missouri, makes more than $80,000 a year, owns her own home in a suburb of Kansas City, and has a master's in business administration from Harvard University. A lifelong Missourian, Mary has no desire to relocate and has expressed several times during the training that she has no interest in marrying or relocating, or in becoming involved in a long-term intimate relationship.

Mary seems very authentic, has clearly done her homework about the child welfare system, and seems ready to parent. But there is something about her that you cannot quite put your finger on. It seems as though she is holding back some information, and the more you develop a relationship with her, the less clear it becomes.

- How do you proceed?
- Do you think sexual orientation is an issue; if so or if not, how do you proceed?

AFFIRMING POLICIES FROM NATIONAL ORGANIZATIONS

CWLA's (2005) Position Statement on Parenting of Children by Gay, Lesbian, and Bisexual Adults

CWLA's Position on Same-Sex Parenting

The Child Welfare League of America (CWLA) affirms that gay, lesbian, and bisexual parents are as well suited to raise children as their heterosexual counterparts.

Issue

Among its member agencies, CWLA also values and encourages approaches to child welfare that are culturally competent and responsive to the specific needs of our society's broad and diverse population. Included in CWLA's definition of cultural competence is the ability to support children, youth, and families who are gay, lesbian, bisexual, or transgender (GLBT), as well as those individuals who may be questioning (Q) their sexual orientation or gender identity.

Based on more than three decades of social science research and our 85 years of service to millions of families, CWLA believes that families with GLBTQ members deserve the same levels of support afforded other families. Any attempt to preclude or prevent gay, lesbian, and bisexual individuals or couples from parenting, based solely on their sexual orientation, is not in the best interest of children.

CWLA, therefore, affirms that gay, lesbian, and bisexual parents are as well suited to raise children as their heterosexual counterparts.

CWLA Standards Support Same-Sex Parenting

As they pertain to GLBTQ children, youth, and families, CWLA's *Standards of Excellence for Family Foster Care Services* do not include requirements for adults present in the home to be legally related by blood, adoption, or legal marriage. Specifically, Section 3.18 of the foster care standards establishes a policy of nondiscrimination in the selection of foster parents, stating: "The family foster care agency should not reject foster parent applicants solely due to their age, income, marital status, race, religious preference, sexual orientation, physical or disabling condition, or location of the foster home" (CWLA, 1995).

CWLA also articulates a strong position on the issue of nondiscrimination of adoptive applicants. Section 4.7 of the *Standards of Excellence for Adoption Services* states:

All applicants should be assessed on the basis of their abilities to successfully parent a child needing family membership and not on their race, ethnicity or culture, income, age, marital status, religion, appearance, differing lifestyle, or sexual orientation. Applicants should be accepted on the basis of an individual assessment of their capacity to understand and meet the needs of a particular available child at the point of the adoption and in the future (CWLA, 2000).

The Child Welfare League of America's *Standards for Adoption Services of Excellenc* (2000) address the issue of sexual orientation of applicants in the following sections:

> All applicants should have an equal opportunity to apply for the consideration of their qualifications as adoptive parents, under applicable law. (5.4) Applicants should be fairly assessed on their abilities to successfully parent a child needing family membership and not on their appearance, differing lifestyle, or sexual preference. (5.4) Agencies should assess each applicant from the perspective of what would be in the best interest of the child. The interest of the child is paramount. (5.4) Sexual preference should not be the sole criteria on which the suitability of the adoptive applicants is based. Consideration should be given to other personality and maturity factors and on the ability of the applicant to meet the specific needs of the individual child. (5.8) The needs of the child are the priority consideration in adoption.

Gay/lesbian adoptive applicants should be assessed the same as any other adoptive applicant. It should be recognized that sexual orientation and the capacity to nurture a child are separate issues. Staff and board training on cultural diversity should include factual information about gay men and lesbians as potential adoptive resources for children needing families in order to dispel common myths about gay men and lesbians.

Gay and lesbian applicants should be informed that biological parents are told about potential adoptive parents for their child, including the sexual orientation of the prospective adoptive parent(s). Some biological parents many choose not to consider gay or lesbian families and agencies usually follow the expressed wishes of the parent. For additional information see Kreisher (2002) at http://www.cwla.org/articles/cv0201gayadopt.htm.

Statement of the American Psychological Association Regarding Discrimination Against Homosexuals: Adopted January 1975 (Paige, 2005)

The American Psychological Association (APA) supports the action taken on December 15, 1973, by the American Psychiatric Association, removing homosexuality from that Association's official list of mental disorders. The American Psychological Association therefore adopts the following resolution:

Homosexuality per se implies no impairment in judgment, stability, reliability, or general social and vocational capabilities. Further, the American Psychological Association urges all mental health professionals to take the lead in removing the stigma of mental illness that has long been associated with homosexual orientations.

Regarding discrimination against homosexuals, the American Psychological Association adopts the following resolution concerning their civil and legal rights:

The American Psychological Association deplores all public and private discrimination in such areas as employment, housing, public accommodation, and licensing against those who engage in or have engaged in homosexual activities and declares that no burden of proof of such judgment, capacity, or reliability shall by placed upon these individuals greater than that imposed on any other persons. Further, the American Psychological Association supports and urges the enactment of civil rights legislation at the local, State, and Federal level that would offer citizens who engage in acts of homosexuality the same protections now guaranteed to others on the basis of race, creed, color, etc. Further, the American Psychological Association supports and urges the repeal of all discriminatory legislation singling out homosexual acts by consenting adults in private.

At its September 1976 meeting, the Task Force on the Status of Lesbian and Gay Psychologists of the Board of Social and Ethical Responsibility for Psychology of the American Psychology Association adopted the following position: "The sex, gender identity, or sexual orientation of natural or prospective adoptive or foster parents should not be the sole or primary variable considered in custody or placement."

Statement of the National Association of Social Workers' Code of Ethics on Gay and Lesbian Issues (1996)

Social workers should not practice, condone, facilitate, or collaborate with any form of discrimination on the basis of race, color, sex, sexual orientation, age, religion, national origin, marital status, political belief, mental or physical handicap, or any other preference or personal characteristic, condition, or status.

Social workers should act to prevent and eliminate discrimination against any person or group on the basis of race, color, sex, sexual orientation, age, religion, national origin, marital status, political belief, mental or physical handicap, or preference or personal characteristic, condition, or status.

Social workers should act to expand choice and opportunity for all persons, with special regard to disadvantaged or oppressed groups and persons.

National Association of Social Workers

The National Association of Social Workers (2002) approved the following policy statement in August 2002 at the their Delegate Assembly:

Legislation legitimizing second-parent adoptions in same-sex households should be supported. Legislation seeking to restrict foster care and adoption by gay, lesbian, bisexual or transgender people should be vigorously opposed.

North American Council on Adoptable Children

The North American Council on Adoptable Children (2002) issued a policy statement that states:

Everyone with the potential to successfully parent a child in foster care and adoption is entitled to fair and equal consideration regardless of sexual orientation or differing life style or physical appearance.

National Association of Foster Parents

The National Association of Foster Parents has not issued a policy statement and has not taken an official position on gay and lesbian foster parents.

American Psychiatric Association

The American Psychiatric Association adopted the following position statement at its November 2002 meeting:

> The American Psychiatric Association supports initiatives that allow same-sex couples to adopt and co-parent children and supports all the associated legal rights, benefits, and responsibilities which arise from such initiatives.

The American Psychiatric Association adopted the following position statement at its December 1997 meeting:

1. Sexual orientation should not be used as the sole or primary factor in child custody decisions.
2. Gay and lesbian couples and individuals should be allowed to become parents through adoption, fostering and new reproductive technologies, subject to the same type of screening used with heterosexual couples and individuals.
3. Second-parent adoptions which grant full parental rights to a second, unrelated adult (usually an unmarried partner of a legal parent), are often in the best interest of the child(ren) and should not be prohibited solely because both adults are of the same gender.
4. Custody determinations after dissolution of a gay relationship should be done in a manner similar to other custody determinations.

American Academy of Pediatrics

The American Academy of Pediatrics (2002b) issued the following statement in support of gay and lesbian parenting and called for equal access to co-parenting and second-parent adoption rights for gay and lesbian parents:

> Children deserve to know that their relationships with both of their parents are stable and legally recognized. This applies

to all children, whether their parents are of the same or opposite sex. The American Academy of Pediatrics recognizes that a considerable body of professional literature provides evidence that children with parents who are homosexual can have the same advantages and the same expectations for health, adjustment, and development as can children whose parents are heterosexual. When 2 adults participate in parenting a child, they and the child deserve the serenity that comes with legal recognition.

Children born or adopted into families headed by partners who are of the same sex usually have only 1 biologic or adoptive legal parent. The other partner in a parental role is called the "coparent" or "second parent." Because these families and children need the permanence and security that are provided by having 2 fully sanctioned and legally defined parents, the Academy supports the legal adoption of children by coparents or second parents. Denying legal parent status through adoption to coparents or second parents prevents these children from enjoying the psychologic and legal security that comes from having 2 willing, capable, and loving parents.

Coparent or second-parent adoption protects the child's right to maintain continuing relationships with both parents. The legal sanction provided by coparent adoption accomplishes the following:

1. Guarantees that the second parent's custody rights and responsibilities will be protected if the first parent were to die or become incapacitated. Moreover, second-parent adoption protects the child's legal right of relationships with both parents. In the absence of coparent adoption, members of the family of the legal parent, should he or she become incapacitated, might successfully challenge the surviving coparent's rights to continue to parent the child, thus causing the child to lose both parents.

2. Protects the second parent's rights to custody and visitation if the couple separates. Likewise, the child's right to maintain relationships with both parents after separation, viewed as important to a positive outcome in separation or

divorce of heterosexual parents, would be protected for families with gay or lesbian parents.

3. Establishes the requirement for child support from both parents in the event of the parents' separation.

4. Ensures the child's eligibility for health benefits from both parents.

5. Provides legal grounds for either parent to provide consent for medical care and to make education, health care, and other important decisions on behalf of the child.

6. Creates the basis for financial security for children in the event of the death of either parent by ensuring eligibility to all appropriate entitlements, such as Social Security survivors benefits.

On the basis of the acknowledged desirability that children have and maintain a continuing relationship with 2 loving and supportive parents, the Academy recommends that pediatricians do the following:

- Be familiar with professional literature regarding gay and lesbian parents and their children.

- Support the right of every child and family to the financial, psychological, and legal security that results from having legally recognized parents who are committed to each other and to the welfare of their children.

- Advocate for initiatives that establish permanency through coparent or second-parent adoption for children of same-sex partners through the judicial system, legislation, and community education.

American Psychoanalytic Association

The American Psychoanalytic Association (2002) adopted this policy statement in support of gay and lesbian parenting:

> The American Psychoanalytic Association supports the position that the salient consideration in decisions about parenting, including conception, child rearing, adoption, visitation and custody is the best interest of the child. Accumulated

evidence suggests the best interest of the child requires attachment to committed, nurturing and competent parents. Evaluation of an individual or couple for these parental qualities should be determined without prejudice regarding sexual orientation. Gay and lesbian individuals and couples are capable of meeting the best interest of the child and should be afforded the same rights and should accept the same responsibilities as heterosexual parents. With the adoption of this position statement, we support research studies that further our understanding of the impact of both traditional and gay/lesbian parenting on a child's development.

American Bar Association

The American Bar Association (1995) adopted the following position statement in August 2003:

> RESOLVED, That the American Bar Association supports state and territorial laws and court decisions that permit the establishment of legal parent-child relationships through joint adoptions and second-parent adoptions by unmarried persons who are functioning as a child's parents when such adoptions are in the best interests of the child.

The association adopted the following position statement in February 1999:

> RESOLVED, that the American Bar Association supports the enactment of laws and implementation of public policy that provide that sexual orientation shall not be a bar to adoption when the adoption is determined to be in the best interest of the child.

The American Bar Association adopted the following position statement in August 1995:

> BE IT RESOLVED, that the American Bar Association supports the enactment of legislation and implementation of public policy providing that child custody and visitation shall not be denied or restricted on the basis of sexual orientation.

American Medical Association

The American Medical Association (2004) adopted the following position statement at its June 2004 meeting:

Whereas, Having two fully sanctioned and legally defined parents promotes a safe and nurturing environment for children, including psychological and legal security; and

Whereas, Children born or adopted into families headed by partners who are of the same sex usually have only one biologic or adoptive legal parent; and

Whereas, The legislative protection afforded to children of parents in homosexual relationships varies from state to state, with some states enacting or considering legislation sanctioning co-parent or second parent adoption by partners of the same sex, several states declining to consider legislation, and at least one state altogether banning adoption by the second parent; and

Whereas, Co-parent or second parent adoption guarantees that the second parent's custody rights and responsibilities are protected if the first parent dies or becomes incapacitated; and

Whereas, Co-parent or second parent adoption ensures the child's eligibility for health benefits from both parents and establishes the requirement for child support from both parents in the event of the parents' separation; and

Whereas, Co-parent or second parent adoption establishes legal grounds to provide consent for medical care and to make health care decisions on behalf of the child and guarantees visitation rights if the child becomes hospitalized; and

Whereas, The American Academy of Pediatrics and the American Psychiatric Association have each issued statements supporting initiatives which allow same-sex couples to adopt and co-parent children; therefore be it

RESOLVED, That our American Medical Association support legislative and other efforts to allow the adoption of a child by the same-sex partner, or opposite sex non-married partner, who functions as a second parent or co-parent to that child.

American Academy of Family Physicians

The American Academy of Family Physicians adopted the following position statement at its October 2002 meeting:

R ESOLVED, That the AAFP establish policy and be supportive of legislation which promotes a safe and nurturing environment, including psychological and legal security, for all children, including those of adoptive parents, regardless of the parents' sexual orientation. (Gloor, Porter, & Stoever, 2002)

American Academy of Child and Adolescent Psychiatry

The American Academy of Child and Adolescent Psychiatry approved the following statement in support of gay, lesbian, and bisexual people in June 1999:

T he basis on which all decisions relating to custody and parental rights should rest on the best interest of the child. Lesbian, gay, and bisexual individuals historically have faced more rigorous scrutiny than heterosexuals regarding their rights to be or become parents.

There is no evidence to suggest or support that parents with a gay, lesbian, or bisexual orientation are per se different from or deficient in parenting skills, child-centered concerns and parent-child attachments, when compared to parents with a heterosexual orientation. It has long been established that a homosexual orientation is not related to psychopathology, and there is no basis on which to assume that a parental homosexual orientation will increase likelihood of or induce a homosexual orientation in the child.

Outcome studies of children raised by parents with a homosexual or bisexual orientation, when compared to heterosexual parents, show no greater degree of instability in the parental relationship or developmental dysfunction in children.

The AACAP opposes any discrimination based on sexual orientation against individuals in regard to their rights as custodial or adoptive parents as adopted by Council.

WEB RESOURCES

COLAGE (Children of Lesbians and Gays Everywhere!)

www.colage.org

COLAGE is by and for children of LGBT parents. COLAGE engages, connects with, and empowers people to make the world a better place for children of LGBT parents and families. COLAGE envisions a world in which all families are valued, protected, reflected, and embraced by society and all of its institutions; in which all children grow up loved and nurtured by kinship networks and communities that teach them about, connect them to, and honor their unique heritage; and in which every human being has the freedom to express sexual orientation, gender identity, and self.

COLAGE envisions a world in which people with LGBT parents or families are connected to a broad community of peers and mentors, are recognized as the authority of our experiences, belong to respected and valued family structures, and have the tools and support to create a just society.

Families Like Ours

www.familieslikeours.org

Families Like Ours is the premier national nonprofit group providing adoption resources to preadoptive and postadoptive families, foster families, and adoption professionals, 24 hours a day, seven days a week. Families Like Ours supports all families wishing to adopt. Although its emphasis is on gay and lesbian adoptive families, Families Like Ours welcomes all families regardless of sexual orientation and family structure.

Family Pride Coalition

www.familypride.org

Across the country and around the world, groups of lesbian and gay parents and families gather to socialize, educate, support, and advocate for children and families. These are known as local parenting groups, and the Family Pride Coalition supports them. Many groups include LGBT individuals and couples who are considering parenthood. Each parenting group has a unique personality influenced by its geographic location, its political climate, and the needs of the families involved. Also shaping the character of the group are the goals and objectives of the group's leadership. Almost without exception, volunteers organize and run these groups. Some have flourished for years; others are brand new. All of them are important. Many groups have been created with the support and assistance of Family Pride, although many groups spontaneously appear. Parenting groups may consist of a few parents who meet monthly for potluck dinners or clusters of families who write letters to their school boards in behalf of creating diverse and inclusive curriculum. Some parenting groups might organize major events and conferences for the LGBT parenting community, whereas others focus on recreational activities. Some groups produce newsletters and monthly mailings. Some groups are led by steering committees, and some have no defined structure. Some groups are even nonprofit organizations with boards of directors. Whatever the size and focus of the group, they are all created by parents and families who share stories, support, and the work of keeping their group alive. These local groups are listed on the familypride.org website, state by state.

Gay.com

Gay.com has a wonderful website that assists lesbian and gay men considering parenthood. See the document is entitled "Paths to Parenting: Family Building Options" at http://www.gay.com/families/article.html?sernum=385.

Gay Parent Magazine

http://www.gayparentmag.com/

Gay Parent magazine is a 16-page bound newsprint magazine featuring personal stories of LGBT parents from across the country and around the world. Parents speak candidly about their experiences with international and domestic adoption, foster care, donor insemination, using a surrogate, and what it is like to raise their children in their part of the world.

Gay Parent provides resources on gay-friendly private schools, day and overnight camps, and family vacation ideas. Resources also include family-building help, such as reproductive technology information and adoption and foster care agencies. Book reviews, news, activities, and events pertaining to LGBT parents and their children are features. On *Gay Parent*'s website, view sample articles, gay-friendly advertisers, advertising rate information, and support groups, and order a subscription or back issue.

Lambda Legal Defense and Education Fund

www.lambdalegal.org

Lambda Legal provides legal advice and support for people experiencing sexual orientation–based harassment and other discrimination. Lambda Legal has a special project that focuses on foster care issues and has a longstanding interest in lesbian and gay adoption issues.

National Center for Lesbian Rights (NCLR)

http://www.nclrights.org/publications/adptn0204.htm

NCLR is a national legal resource center with a primary commitment to advancing the rights and safety of lesbians and their families through a program of litigation, public policy advocacy, and public education. In addition, NCLR provides representation and resources to gay men and bisexual and transgender individuals on key issues that also significantly advance lesbian rights. NCLR has a wonderful summary of lesbian and gay parenting issues, which can be found on its website.

PFLAG (Parents, Families and Friends of Lesbians and Gays)

www.pflag.org

PFLAG celebrates diversity and envisions a society that embraces everyone, including those of diverse sexual orientations and gender identities. Only with respect, dignity, and equality for all will we reach our full potential as human beings, individually and collectively. PFLAG welcomes the participation and support of all who share in and hope to realize this vision.

PFLAG promotes the health and well-being of LGBT people, their families, and their friends through support to cope with an adverse society, education to enlighten an ill-informed public, and advocacy to end discrimination and secure equal civil rights. PFLAG provides an opportunity for dialogue about sexual orientation and gender identity and works to create a healthy society that is respectful of human diversity.

PrideLinks

www.pridelinks.com

This website includes a plethora of resources on lesbian and gay parenting.

VIDEO RESOURCES

Daddy & Papa

Daddy & Papa is a one-hour documentary exploring the personal, cultural, and political effect of gay men who are making a decision that is at once traditional and revolutionary: raising children themselves. Taking us inside four gay male families, *Daddy & Papa* traces the day-to-day challenges and the larger, critical issues that inevitably intersect their private lives—the ambiguous place of inter-racial families in America, the wonder and precariousness of surrogacy and adop-tion, the complexities of marriage and divorce in the gay community, and the legality of their own parenthood. To purchase a copy of this video, contact http://daddyandpapa.com/order.html.

Choosing Children: A Film About Lesbians Becoming Parents (1985)

This film provides an intimate look at the issues faced by women who become parents after coming out as lesbians. Six families share their experiences with donor insemination, nonbiological motherhood, adoption, and other issues. For more information, contact Cambridge Documentary Films, P.O. Box 385, Cambridge, MA 02139, 617/354-3677.

Making Babies: The Gay and Lesbian Baby Boom (1997)

This film is a sweet, touching look at four gay and lesbian couples in Los Angeles as they create their families through foster parenting, adoption, and intrauterine insemination. For more information, call 213/650-7497.

Paternal Instinct (2005)

Mark and Erik have been together for 10 years, and they have decided it is time to have kids, but they do not want to adopt. Is there a woman out there willing to serve as a surrogate mother and help them realize their dream? This film chronicles two years in the life of these New Yorkers on their journey to become fathers. To order this film, visit http://www.paternalinstinctfilm.com/.

REFERENCES

Achtenberg, R. (1990). *Preserving and protecting the families of lesbian and gay men.* San Francisco: Nation Center for Lesbian Rights.

Adopt US Kids. (2004). *Answering the call.* Baltimore: Author.

Adoption of Tammy. 416 Mass. 205, 619 NE2d 315 (1993).

Agigian, A. (2004). *Baby steps: How lesbian alternative insemination is changing the world.* Wesleyan, CT: Wesleyan University Press.

Allen, M., & Burrell, N. (1996). Comparing the impact of homosexual and heterosexual parents on children: Meta-analysis of existing research. *Journal of Homosexuality, 32,* 19–35.

American Academy of Child and Adolescent Psychiatry. (1999). *Policy statement: Gay, lesbian, and bisexual parents.* Retrieved May 12, 2006, from http://www.aacap.org/publications/policy/ps46.htm.

American Academy of Pediatrics. (2002a, February 4). *Press release: AAP says children of same-sex couples deserve two legally recognized parents,* Retrieved May 8, 2006, from http://www.aap.org/advocacy/archives/febsamesex.htm.

American Academy of Pediatrics. (2002b, February). Technical report: Coparent or second-parent adoption by same-sex parents. *Pediatrics, 109,* 341–344.

American Bar Assocation. (1995). *Recommendation.* Retrieved May 12, 2006, from http://www.abanet.org/leadership/2006/midyear/daily_journal/102.doc.

American Civil Liberties Union. (2005). *Gay rights project.* Available from www.aclu.org.

American Medical Assocation. (n.d.). *AMA policy regarding sexual orientation.* Retrieved May 12, 2006, from http://www.ama-assn.org/ama/pub/category/14754.html.

American Psychiatric Association. (1968). *Diagnostic and statistical manual of mental disorders II.* Washington, DC: Author.

American Psychiatric Association. (2000, May). *Gay, lesbian and bisexual issues.* Retrieved May 8, 2006, from http://healthyminds.org/glbissues.cfm.

American Psychiatric Association. (2002). *Adoption and co-parenting by same sex couples.* Retrieved May 12, 2006, from http://www.psych.org/edu/other_res/lib_archives/archives/ 200214.pdf.

American Psychoanalytic Assocation. (2002). *Principles and standards of ethics for psychoanalysts.* Retrieved May 8, 2006, from http://apsa.org/ethicscode.pdf.

Anderson, G., Ryan, C., Taylor-Brown, S., & White-Gray, M. (Eds.). (1999). *Children and HIV/AIDS.* New Brunswick, NJ: Transactions.

Appleby, G., & Anastas, J. (1998). *Not just a passing phase: Social work with gay, lesbian and bisexual persons.* New York: Columbia University Press.

Arizona law gives gay foster parents edge. (1997, November 13). *Phoenix Times,* A3.

Arnold, T. (1997, July 16). Protect foster kids from gay discrimination. *Edmonton Journal,* 31.

Baldauf, S. (1997, December 3). How Texas wrestles with gay adoptions. *Christian Science Monitor,* 3.

Baby M, 537 A.2d 1227, 109 N.J. 396 (N.J., 1988, February 3).

Baker, P. (1997, November 20). Clinton signs law to speed adoption process for children in foster care. *Washington Post,* p. A17.

Barbell, K., & Sheikh, L. (2000). *A community outreach handbook for recruiting foster parents.* Washington, DC: Child Welfare League of America.

Barret, R., & Robinson, B. E. (2000). *Gay fathers.* New York: Jossey-Bass.

Benkov, L. (1994). *Reinventing the family: The emerging story of lesbian and gay parents.* New York: Crown.

Bernfeld, R. (1995). A brief guide regarding donor and co-parenting agreements. In M. E. Elovitz & C. Schneider (Eds.), *Legal issues facing the nontraditional family—1995* (pp. 135–169). New York: Practicing Law Institute.

Bigner, J. (1996). Working with gay fathers. In J. Laird & R.-J. Green (Eds.), *Lesbians and gays in couples and families: A handbook for therapists* (pp. 370–403). San Francisco: Jossey-Bass.

Bigner, J. J., & Jacobsen, R. R. (1989a). Parenting behaviors of homosexual and heterosexual fathers. *Journal of Homosexuality, 18,* 173–186.

Bigner, J. J., & Jacobsen, R. R. (1989b). The value of children for gay versus nongay fathers. *Journal of Homosexuality, 18,* 163–172.

Bigner, J. J., & Jacobsen, R. B. (1992). Adult responses to child behavior and attitudes towards fathering: Gay and non-gay fathers. *Journal of Homosexuality, 21,* 173–186.

Bos, H., van Balen, F., & van den Boom, D. (2004). Experience of parenthood, couple relationships, social support, and child-rearing goals in planned lesbian mother families, *Journal of Child Psychology and Psycharatry, 45*(4), 755-764.

Bowers v. Hardwick, 478 U.S. 186, 106 S.Ct. 2841, 92 L.Ed.2d 140 (1986).

Bozett, F. W. (1980). Gay fathers: How and why they disclose their homosexuality to their children. *Family Relations, 29,* 173–179.

Brodzinsky, D. M., & Schechter, M. D. (Eds.). (1990). *The psychology of adoption.* New York: Oxford.

Bozett, F. W. (Ed.). (1987). *Gay and lesbian parents.* New York: Praeger Press.

Brodzinsky, D. M., Schechter, M. D., & Marantz, R. (1993). *Being adopted: The lifelong search for self.* New York: Anchor Books.

Bronston, B. (2004, November 14). Children of same-sex parents fare well in research: Early studies find positive outcomes, but more work remains. *New Orleans Times Picayune,* 14.

Brooks, D., & Goldberg, S. (2001). Gay and lesbian adoptive and foster care placements: Can they meet the needs of waiting children? *Families in Society, 46,* 147–157.

Cameron, P., Cameron, K., & Landess, T. (1996). Errors by the American Psychiatric Association, the American Psychological Association and the National Education Association in representing homosexuality in aminus briefs about Amendment 2 to the U.S. Supreme Court. *Psychological Reports, 79*, 383–404.

Carey, B. (2005, January 29). Experts dispute Bush on gay-adoption issue. *New York Times*, A23.

Cass, V. C. (1979). Homosexual identity formation: A theoretical model. *Journal of Homosexuality, 4*, 219–235.

Cass, V. C. (1984). Homosexual identity formation: Testing a theoretical model. *Journal of Sex Research, 20*, 143–167.

Chan, R. W., Raboy, B., & Patterson, C. J. (2000). Psychosocial adjustment among children conceived via donor insemination by lesbian and heterosexual mothers. *Child Development 69*, 443–457.

Chauncey, G. (1994). *Gay New York: Gender, urban culture, and the making of the gay male world, 1890–1940*. New York: Basic Books.

Child Welfare League of America. (1995). *CWLA standards of excellence for family foster care services*. Washington, DC: CWLA Press.

Child Welfare League of America. (2000). *Standards of excellence for adoption services*. Washington, DC: CWLA Press.

Child Welfare League of America. (n.d.). *Position statement on parenting of children by gay, lesbian, and bisexual adults*. Retrieved May 12, 2006, from http://www.cwla.org/programs/culture/ glbtqposition.htm.

Children's Defense Fund. (2004). *State of America's children yearbook 2004*. Washington, DC: Author.

Coleman, E. (1981). Developmental stages of the coming out process. *Journal of Homosexuality, 7*(2/3), 31–43.

Constant A. v. Paul C.A. 496 A.2d 1 (Pa. Super Ct., 1985).

Cooper, D. (1994). *From darkness into light: What the Bible really says about homosexuality* (3rd ed.) Tucson, AZ: Cornerstone Fellowship.

Cooper, L., and Cates, P. (2006). *Too high a price: The case against restricting gay parenting*. NY: ACLU.

Cosis-Brown, H. (1991). Competent child-focused practice: Working with lesbian and gay parents. *Adopting & Fostering, 15*(2), 11–17.

Cosis-Brown, H. (1992). Gender, sex, and sexuality in the assessment of prospective parents. *Adopting & Fostering, 16*(2), 30–34.

Court refuses challenge to gay foster placements. (1997, October 7). *Boston Globe*, 43.

Craig-Olsen, H., Craig, J. A., & Morton, T. (2006, March/April). Issues of shared parenting of LGBTQ children and youth in foster care: Preparing foster parents for new roles. *Child Welfare, 85*, 267–280.

Cramer, D. (1986). Gay parents and their children: A review of research and practical implications. *Journal of Counseling and Development, 64*, 501–507.

Crary, D. (2006, March 24). Report backs recruiting for gay and lesbian adoptions. *Philadephia Inquirer*, 21.

De Monteflores, C., & Schultz, S. J. (1978). Coming out: Similarities and differences for lesbians and gay men. *Journal of Social Issues, 34*(3), 59–72.

Diller, J. V. (1999). *Cultural diversity: A primer for the human services*. Boston: Brooks/Cole.

Downs, C., & James, S. E. (2006, March/April). Gay, lesbian, and bisexual foster parents: Strengths and challenges for the child welfare system. *Child Welfare, 85*, 281–298.

Dunlap, D. W. (1996, January 7). Homosexual parent raising children: Support for pro and con. *New York Times*, L15.

Elovitz, M. E. (1995). Adoption by lesbian and gay people: The use and misuse of social science research. In M. E. Elovitz & C. Schneider (Eds.), *Legal issues facing the nontraditional family—1995* (pp. 171–191). New York: Practicing Law Institute.

Evan B. Donaldson Adoption Institute. (2003). *Adoption by lesbians and gays: A national survey of adoption agency policies, practices, and attitudes*. New York: Author.

Family Futures Consortium. (2004, April 25). *One-day workshop for gay and lesbian adoptive and fosters parents*. Unpublished paper.

Fanshel, D. (1982). *On the road to permanency: An expanded data base for children in foster care*. New York: Child Welfare League of America.

Fanshel, D., & Shinn, E. (1978). *Children in foster care: A longitudinal investigation*. New York: Columbia University Press.

Feigelman, W., & Silverman, A. S. (1983). *Chosen children: New patterns of adoptive relationships*. New York: Praeger.

Feigelman, W., & Silverman, A. R. (1997). Single parent adoption. In *The handbook for single adoptive parents* (pp. 123–129). Chevy Chase, MD: National Council for Single Adoptive Parents.

Ferrero, E., Freker, J., & Foster, T. (2005). *Too high a price to pay: The case against restricting gay parenting* (2nd ed.). Washington, DC: ACLU.

Festinger, T. (1983). *No one ever asked us: A post script to foster care*. New York: Columbia University Press.

Flaks, D. K. (1994, Summer). Gay and lesbian families: Judicial assumptions, scientific realities. *William & Mary Bill of Rights Journal, 3*(1), 345–372.

Florida judge upholds state gay adoption ban. (1997, July 29). *Miami Herald*, 33.

Forstein, M. (1988). Homophobia: An overview. *Psychiatric Annals, 18*, 33–36.

Freeman, D. (2005, November/December). Finding my father: My dream dad turned out to be gay. *Represent: The Voice of Youth in Care*, 4–8.

Freiberg, P. (1999, January 22). Gay adoption rights under attack. *New York Blade*, 1, 7.

Foucault, M. (1976). *Mental illness and psychology*. New York: Harper and Row.

Freundlich, M., & Wright, L. (2003). *Post-permanency services*. Washington, DC: Casey Family Programs.

Frommer, M. S. (1996). The right fit: A gay man's quest for fatherhood. *In the Family, 2*(1), 12–16, 26.

Garner, A. (2004). *Families like mine: Children of gay parents tell it like it is*. New York: HarperCollins.

Georgia ban on gay adoption in committee. (1998, March 10). *Atlanta Times*, 2.

Gloor, J., Porter, S., & Stoever, J. (2002). *Special constituencies suggest new AAFP policies*. Retrieved May 12, 2006, from http://www.aafp.org/fpr/20020600/4.html.

Goldstein, J., Solnit, A. J., Goldstein, S., & Freud. A. (1996). *The best interest of the child*. New York: Free Press.

Golmbok, S., Perry, B., Burston, A., Murray, C., Mooney-Somers, I. & Stevens, M. (2003). Children with lesbian parents: A community study. *Developmental Psychology, 29*(1), 20-23.

Golombok, S., Spencer, A., & Rutter, M. (1983). Children in lesbian and single-parent households: Psychosexual and psychiatric appraisal. *Journal of Child Psychology and Psychiatry, 24*(4), 551–572.

Golombok, S., & Tasker, F. (1996). Do parents influence the sexual orientation of their children? Findings from a longitudinal study of lesbian families. *Developmental Psychology, 32*(1), 3–11.

Golombok, S., Tasker, F., & Murray, C. (1997). Children raised in fatherless families from infancy: Family relationships and the socioemotional development of children of children of lesbian and single heterosexual mothers. *Journal of Child Psychology and Psychiatry 38*, 783–791.

Green, A. A. (1999, January 7). Board votes to ban gays as providers of foster care. *Arkansas Democratic Gazette*, 1, 5A.

Green, J. (1999). *The velveteen father: An unexpected journey to parenthood.* New York: Villard.

Greene, B. (1994). Lesbian and gay sexual orientations: Implications for clinical training, practice and research. In B. Greene & G. M. Herek (Eds.), *Lesbian and gay psychology: Theory, research, and clinical applications* (pp. 1–24). Thousand Oaks, CA: Sage.

Groninger, T. (1992). *Rethinking recruitment: How to find the families that you want.* Lewisburg, PA: Thomas Groninger Associates.

Groninger, T. (1996, March/April). Foster care recruiting still in the closet. *Youth Today*, 54.

Groth, A. N. (1978). Patterns of sexual assault against children and adolescents. In A. W. Burgess, A. N. Groth, L. L. Holmstrom, & S. M. Sgroi (Eds.), *Sexual assault of children and adolescents* (pp. 220–238). Lexington, MA: Lexington Books.

Groth, A. N., & Birnbaum, H. J. (1978). Adult sexual orientation and attraction to underage persons. *Archives of Sexual Behavior, 7*(3), 175–181.

Groze, V. K., & Rosenthal, J. A. (1991). Single parents and their adopted children: A psychosocial analysis. *Journal of Contemporary Human Services*, 130–139.

Guggenheim, M., Lowe Dylan, A., & Curtis, D. (1996). Gay and lesbian families. In *The rights of families* (pp. 269–294). Carbondale, IL: Southern Illinois University Press.

Harris, F. (2005, November/December). My place in the world. In my new home, I can admit I'm gay. *Represent: The Voice of Youth in Care,* 10–11.

Hartman, A. (1996). Social policy as a context for lesbian and gay families: The political is personal. In J. Laird & R.-J. Green (Eds.), *Lesbians and gays in couples and families: A handbook for therapists* (pp. 69–85). San Francisco: Jossey-Bass.

Hartman, A., & Laird, J. (1983). *Family-centered social work practice.* New York: Free Press.

Hartman, A., & Laird, J. (1998). Moral and ethic issues in working with lesbians and gay men. *Families in Society*, 263–276.

Helminiak, D. A. (1997). *What the Bible really says about homosexuality.* San Francisco: Alamo Square Press.

Hennie, M. A. (1999, January 29). Historic second term may set agenda for presidential bid: Texas Gov. Bush joined the bandwagon opposing gay/lesbian adoption and parenting. *Impact*, 1.

Herek, G. M. (1991). Stigma, prejudice and violence against lesbians and gay men. In J. C. Gonsiorek & J. D. Weinrich (Eds.), *Homosexuality: Research implications for public policy* (pp. 60–80). Newbury Park: Sage.

Herman, D. (1997). *The anti-gay agenda: Orthodox vision and the Christian right.* Chicago: University of Chicago Press.

Hicks, S. (2000). Good lesbian, bad lesbian: Regulating heterosexuality in fostering and adoption assessments. *Child & Family Social Work, 5*, 157–168.

Hicks, S., & McDermott, J. (Eds.). (1999). *Lesbian and gay fostering and adoption: Extraordinary yet ordinary.* London: Jessica Kingsley.

Howey, N., Samuels, E., Cammermeyer, M., & Savage, D. (2000). *Out of the ordinary: Essays on growing up with gay, lesbian, and transgender parents.* New York: Stonewall Inn.

Human Rights Campaign. (2005). *Top stories*. Retrieved May 12, 2006, from www.hrc.org.

Hunter, J., & Schaecher, R. (1987). Stresses on lesbian and gay adolescents in schools. *Social Work in Education, 9*, 180–188.

Hunter, N. D., & Polikoff, N. D. (1976). Custody rights of lesbian mothers: Legal theory and litigation strategy. *Buffalo Law Review, 25*, 691–733.

Jacobson v. Jacobson, 314 N.W. 2d 78 (N.D. 1981).

Jenny, C., Roesler, T. A., & Poyer, K. L. (1994). Are children at risk for sexual abuse by homosexuals? *Pediatrics, 94*(1), 41–44.

JLP(H.) v. D.J.P. 643 SW2d 865, 869 (Mo.App, 1982).

Johnsrude, L. (1997, November 19). Gay mom loses battle for more foster children. *Edmonton Journal, 3*.

Henry J. Kaiser Family Foundation. (2000). *Sex education in America*. Menlo Park, CA: Author.

Kerr, M. (2006, April 18). Anti gay and lesbian adoption bill fails in Arizona Senate. *Tucson Observer*. Retrieved April 20, 2006, from www.tucsonabserver.com.

Kessler, B. (1997, November 11). QL: Texas foster parent and adoption policy. *Dallas Morning News*, 11.

Kinsey, A. C., Pomeroy, W. B., & Martin, C. E. (1948). *Sexual behavior in the human male*. Philadelphia: W. B. Saunders.

Kinsey, A. C., Pomeroy, W. B., Martin, C. E., & Gebhard, P. H. (1953). *Sexual behavior in the human female*. Philadelphia: W. B. Saunders.

Kleber, D. J., Howell, R. J., & Tibbits-Kleber, H. (1986). The impact of homosexuality in child custody cases: A review of the literature. *Bulletin of American Academy Psychiatry and Law, 14*, 81–87.

Kreisher, K. (2002, January). Gay adoption. *Children's Voice*. Retrieved April 27, 2006, from http://www.cwla.org/articles/cv0201gayadopt.htm.

Lamb, M. E. (Ed.). (1986). *The father's role: Applied perspectives*. New York: John Wiley and Sons.

Lamb, M. E. (Ed.). (1987). *The father's role: Cross cultural perspectives*. Hillsdale, NJ: Erlbaum.

Lamb, M. E. (1997). The development of father-infant relationships. In M. E. Lamb (Ed.), *The role of the father in child development* (pp. 104–120). New York: John Wiley and Sons.

Lambda Legal Defense and Education Fund. (1996). *Lesbian & gay men seeking custody and visitation: An overview of the state of the law*. New York: Author.

Lambda Legal Defense and Education Fund. (1997, September 28). *Lesbian & gay parenting: A fact sheet*. New York: Author.

Lambda Legal Defense and Education Fund. (2003). *Lawrence v. Texas*. Retrieved April 27, 2006, from http://www.lambdalegal.org/cgi-bin/iowa/cases/record?record=93.

Lambda Legal Defense and Education Fund. (n.d.). *Antidiscrimination*. Retrieved April 26, 2006, from www.lambdalegal.org/cgi-bin/iowa/issues/record?record=18.

Lancaster, K. (1996). *Keys to parenting an adopted child*. Hauppauge, NY: Barron's.

Lauman, E. O., Gagnon, J. H., Michael, R. T., & Michaels, S. (1994). *The social organization of sexuality: Sexual practices in the U.S.* Chicago: University of Chicago Press.

Leonard, A. S. (2006). Big adoption advance in Indiana. *Gay City, 5*(6). Retrieved April 20, 2006, from www.gaycity.com.

LeVay, S. (1994). *The sexual brain*. Boston: MIT Press.

Liptak, A. (2006, January 21). Maryland judge voids ban on same-sex marriage; State quickly appeals. *New York Times*, B1.

Loehlin, J. C., & McFadden, D. (2003). Otoacoustic emissions, auditory evoked potentials, and traits related to sex and sexual orientation. *Archives of Sexual Behavior, 32*, 115–127.

Lutz, L. (2002). *Recruitment and retention of resource families: The promise and the paradox.* Seattle, WA: Casey Family Programs.

Maas, H. S., & Engler, R. E. (1959). *Children in need of parents.* New York: Columbia University Press.

Mallon, G. P. (1992). Gay and no place to go: Assessing the needs of gay and lesbian adolescents in out-of-home care settings. *Child Welfare, 71*, 547–556.

Mallon, G. P. (1997). Entering into a collaborative search for meaning with gay and lesbian youths in out-of-home care: An empowerment-based model for training child welfare professionals. *Child and Adolescent Social Work Journal, 14*, 427–444.

Mallon, G. P. (1999a). Lesbians and gay men as foster and adoptive parents. In *Let's get this straight: A gay and lesbian affirming approach to child welfare* (pp. 112–131). New York: Columbia University Press.

Mallon, G. P. (1999b). *Let's get this straight: A gay and lesbian affirming approach to child welfare.* New York: Columbia University Press.

Mallon, G. P. (2000). Gay men and lesbians as adoptive parents. *Journal of Gay and Lesbian Social Services, 11*(4), 1–21.

Mallon, G. P. (2004). *Gay men choosing parenthood.* New York: Columbia University Press.

Mallon, G., & Betts, B. (2005). *Recruiting, assessing and retaining lesbian and gay foster and adoptive families: A good practise guide for social workers.* London: British Association of Adoption and Foster Care.

Mallon, G. P. & Leashore, B. (Eds.). (2002). *Contemporary issues in permanency planning.* Washington, DC: Child Welfare League of America.

Maluccio, A. N., Fein, E., & Olmstead, K. A. (1986). *Permanency planning for children: Concepts and methods.* New York: Tavistock.

Malyon, A. K. (1982). Psychotherapeutic implications of internalized homophobia in gay men. *Journal of Homosexuality, 7*(2/3), 59–69.

Marindin, H. (1997). *The handbook for single adoptive parents.* Chevy Chase, MD: Committee for Single Parents.

Martin, A. (1993). *The lesbian and gay parenting handbook: Creating and raising our families.* New York: Harper Perennial.

Matter of Adoption of Evan. NY.431, 583 N.Y.S.2d 997, 153 Misc. 2d 844 (1992).

Matter of Jacob. Roseanne M. A. et al., Appellants. 86 N.Y.2d 651, 660 N.E.2d 397, 636 N.Y.S.2d 716 (1995, November 2).

Matthews, J. D., & Cramer, E. P. (2006, March/April). Envisioning the adoption process to strengthen gay and lesbian headed families: Recommendations for adoption professionals. *Child Welfare, 85*, 317–340.

Mayfield, W. (2001). The development of an internalized homonegativity inventory for gay men. *Journal of Homosexuality, 41*(2), 53–76.

McFarland, E. (1998, August 26). Foster care ban still sought for gays but not singles. *Arkansas Democratic Gazette*, 1B.

McGarry, K. (2004). *Fatherhood for gay men: An emotional and practical guide to becoming a gay dad.* New York: Haworth Press.

McPherson, D. (1993). *Gay parenting couples: Parenting arrangements, arrangement satisfaction, and relationship satisfaction.* Unpublished doctoral dissertation, Pacific Graduate School of Psychology, Palo Alto, CA.

Melina, L. R. (1998). *Raising adopted children*. New York: Quill.

Meltsner, S. (1987a). *Getting ready to recruit*. Chicago: Jacob Sprouse.

Meltsner, S. (1987b). *Organizing recruitment efforts*. Chicago: Jacob Sprouse.

Menichiello, M. (2006). *A gay couple's journey through surrogacy: Intended fathers,* NY: Haworth Press.

Metropolitan Community Church. (1990). *Homosexuality not a sin, not a sickness: What the Bible does and does not say*. Los Angeles: Author.

Mitchell, V. (1996). Two moms: Contribution of the planned lesbian family and the deconstruction of gendered parenting. In J. Laird & R.-J. Green (Eds.), *Lesbians and gays in couples and families: A handbook for therapists* (pp. 343–357). San Francisco: Jossey-Bass.

Morales, E. S. (1989). Ethnic minority families and minority gays and lesbians. *Marriage and Family Review, 14*, 217–239.

Morrow, D. F., & Messinger, L. (2006). *Sexual orientation and gender expression in social work practice: Working with gay, lesbian, bisexual, and transgender people*. New York: Columbia University Press.

Muzio, C. (1993). Lesbian co-parenting: On being/being the invisible (m)other. *Smith College Studies in Social Work, 63*, 215–229.

Muzio, C. (1996). Lesbians choosing children: Creating families, creating narratives. In J. Laird & R. J. Green (Eds.), *Lesbians and gays in couples and families: A handbook for therapists* (pp. 358–369). San Francisco: Jossey-Bass.

National Adoption Information Clearinghouse. (2004). Latest U.S. adoption statistics show increase in public agency adoptions, while total numbers remain constant. *Children's Bureau Express, 5*(10). Retrieved April 28, 2006, from http://cbexpress.acf.hhs.gov/ nonissart.cfm?issue_id=2004-12&disp_art=881&hlt=1.

National Association of Social Workers. (1996). *Code of ethics*. Washington, DC: NASW Press. Retrieved May 8, 2006, from http://www.naswdc.org/pubs/code/default.asp.

National Association of Social Workers. (2002). *Social work speaks* (7th ed.). Retrieved May 12, 2006, from http://www.naswpress.org/publications/books/policy/sw_speaks/3703.html.

National Commission on Children. (2005). *Sec. 1320b-9*. Retrieved May 4, 2006, from http://www.washingtonwatchdog.org/documents/usc/ttl42/ch7/subchXI/ptA/sec1320b-9.html.

Nelson, N. (1997). *When gay and lesbian people adopt*. Seattle, WA: Northwest Adoption Exchange.

Newton, D. E. (1978). Homosexual behavior and child molestation: A review of the evidence. *Adolescence, 13*, 205–215.

North American Council on Adoptable Children. (2000). *Policy statements: Gay and lesbian foster and adoptive parenting*. Retrieved May 8, 2006, from http://www.nacac.org/pub_statements.html#Gay.

Office of the Inspector General. (2002a). *Recruiting foster parents*. Washington, DC: Office of the Inspector General, U.S. Department of Health and Human Services.

Office of the Inspector General. (2002b). *Retaining foster parents*. Washington, DC: Office of the Inspector General, U.S. Department of Health and Human Services.

OK With It All. (2005, November/December). A gay foster dad opens his home. *Represent: The Voice of Youth in Care,* 12–13.

Osman, S. (1972). My stepfather is a she. *Family Process, 11*, 209–218.

Pace, P. R. (2006, February). Court upholds gay foster parents. *NASW News*, 5.

Paige, R. U. (2005). *Proceedings of the American Psychological Association, Incorporated, for the legislative year 2004. Minutes of the meeting of the Council of Representatives July 28 & 30, 2004, Honolulu, HI.* Retrieved May 12, 2006, from http://www.apa.org/pi/lgbc/policy/parents.html.

Parents & Friends of Lesbians and Gays. (1997). *Beyond the Bible: Parents, families and friends talk about religion and homosexuality.* Washington, DC: Author.

Patterson, C. J. (1992). Children of gay and lesbian parents. *Child Development, 63,* 1025–1042.

Patterson, C. J. (1994). Lesbian and gay couples considering parenthood: An agenda for research, service and advocacy. In L. A. Kurdek (Ed.), *Social services for gay and lesbian couples* (pp. 33–56). New York: Harrington Park Press.

Patterson, C. J. (1995). Lesbian mothers, gay fathers, and their children. In A. R. D'Augelli & C. J. Patterson (Eds.), *Gay, lesbian, and bisexual identities over the lifespan* (pp. 262–292). Oxford, UK: Oxford University Press.

Patterson, C. J. (1996). Lesbian mothers and their children: Findings from the Bay Area families study. In J. Laird & R.-J. Green (Eds.), *Lesbians and gays in couples and families: A handbook for therapists* (pp. 420–438). San Francisco: Jossey-Bass.

Patterson, C. J., Hurt, S., & Mason, C. D. (1998). Families of the lesbian baby-boom: Children's contact with grandparents and other adults. *American Journal of Orthopsychiatry, 68,* 390–399.

Pavao, J. M. (2005). *The family of adoption.* Boston: Beacon.

Pelton, L. H. (1991). Beyond permanency planning: Restructuring the public child welfare system. *Social Work, 36,* 337–44.

Pierce, W. (1992). Adoption and other permanency considerations. *Children and Youth Services Review, 14*(1/2), 61–66.

Pies, C. (1985). *Considering parenthood: A workbook for lesbians.* San Francisco: Spinsters/Aunt Lute.

Pies, C. (1990). Lesbians and the choice to parent. In F. W. Bozett & M. B. Sussman (Eds.), *Homosexuality and family relations* (pp. 138–150). New York: Harrington Park Press.

Polikoff, N. (1986). Lesbian mothers, lesbian families: Legal obstacles, legal challenges. *Review of Law and Social Change, 14,* 907–914.

Pollack, J. S. (1995). *Lesbian & gay families: Redefining parenting in America.* New York: Franklin Watts.

Quinton, D., Rushton, A., Dance, C., & Mayes, D. (1998). *Joining new families: A study of adoption and fostering in middle childhood.* Bristol, UK: University of Bristol and the Institute of Psychiatry.

Raymond, D. (1992). "In the best interest of the child": Thoughts on homophobia and parenting. In W. Blumenfeld (Ed.), *Homophobia: How we all pay the price* (pp. 114–130). Boston: Beacon Press.

Ricketts, W. (1991). *Lesbians and gay men as foster parents.* Portland, MN: University of Southern Maine.

Ricketts, W., & Achtenberg, R. A. (1987). The adoptive and foster gay and lesbian parent. In F. W. Bozett (Ed.), *Gay and lesbian parents* (pp. 89–111). New York: Praeger Press.

Ricketts, W., & Achtenberg, R. A. (1990). Adoption and foster parenting for lesbians and gay men: Creating new traditions in family. *Marriage and Family Review, 14*(3/4), 83–118.

Rivera, R. R. (1987). Legal issues in gay and lesbian parenting. In F. W. Bozett (Ed.), *Gay and lesbian parents* (pp. 199–230). Westport, CT: Praeger.

Roscoe, W. (1987). Living the sprit tradition: Gay American Indians. In M. Thompson (Ed.), *Gay spirit: myth and meaning* (pp. 69–77). New York: St. Martin's Press.

Ryan, S. D. (2000). Examining social workers' placement recommendations of children with gay and lesbian adoptive parents. *Families in Society, 81,* 517–528.

Savage, D. (1999). *The kid (What happened after my boyfriend and I decided to go get pregnant)*. New York: Dutton.

Savic, I., Berglund, H., & Lindström, P. (2005). Brain response to putative pheromones in homosexual men. *National Academy of Science, 102,* 7356–7361.

Savin-Williams, R. C., & Rodriguez, R. G. (1993). A developmental clinical perspective on lesbian, gay male and bisexual youth. In T. P. Gullotta, G. R. Adams, & R. Montemayor (Eds.), *Adolescent sexuality: Advances in adolescent development, Volume 5* (pp. 77–101). Newbury Park, CA: Sage.

Sbordone, A. J. (1993). *Gay men choosing fatherhood.* Unpublished doctoral dissertation. Department of Psychology, City University of New York.

Scott, S. (2002). *Research briefing: The impact on children of having lesbian or gay parents.* London: Barnardo's.

Sellick, C., & Thoburn, J. (1996). *What works in family placement?* London: Barnardo's.

Sexual orientation and the law. (1989). In *Harvard law review.* Cambridge, MA: Harvard University Press.

Shernoff, M. (1996). Gay men choosing to be fathers. In M. Shernoff (Ed.), *Human services for gay people: Clinical and community practice* (pp. 41–54). New York: Harrington Park.

Shidlo, A. (1994). Internalized homophobia: Conceptual and empirical issues in measurement. In B. Greene & G. M. Herek (Eds.), *Psychological perspectives on lesbian and gay issues: Vol. 1: Lesbian and gay psychology: Theory, research, and clinical applications* (pp. 176–205). Thousand Oaks, CA: Sage.

Shorteo, R. (2005, June 19). What's the movement to outlaw gay marriage really about? *New York Times Magazine,* 34–41, 64–67.

Shuster, S. (2005). Can we speak freely? What research has told us about LGBT parenting. *In the Family, 10*(4), 14–17.

Skeates, J., & Jabri, D. (Eds.). (1988). *Fostering and adoption by lesbians and gay men.* London: London Strategic Policy Unit.

Smith, E. P., & Gutheil, R. H. (1988). Successful foster parent recruiting: A voluntary agency effort. *Child Welfare, 67,* 137–146.

Smith, T. (2006, January 20). Legislators reject new birth-certificate rules: Bill would have limited same-sex couples who adopt children in Virginia. *Times-Dispatch,* A13.

Smothers, R. (1997a, December 18). Accord lets gay couples adopt jointly. *New York Times,* B4.

Smothers, R. (1997b, October, 23). Court lets two gay men jointly adopt child. *New York Times,* B5.

Smothers, R. (1998, June 22). Church blesses union of 2 men in adoption case. *New York Times,* B5.

Snow, J. E. (2004). *How it feels to have a gay or lesbian parent: A book by kids for kids of all ages.* New York: Harrington Park Press.

Solot, D. (1998). *Guidelines for adoption workers: Writing lesbian, gay, bisexual, and transgender homestudies for special needs adoptions.* Springfield, VA: Adoption Resource Exchange for Single Parents.

Stacey, J., & Biblarz, T. (2001). (How) Does the sexual orientation of parents matter? *American Sociological Review, 66,* 159–183.

Stein, T. J. (1991). *Child welfare and the law.* New York: Longman.

Stein, T. J. (1996, September). Child custody and visitation: The rights of lesbian and gay parents. *Social Service Review, 35,* 435–450.

Stein, T. J. (1998). *Child welfare and the law* (Rev. ed.). Washington, DC: Child Welfare League of America.

Stepfamily Association of America. (2005). *Stepfamily facts*. Retrieved May 4, 2006, from http://www.saafamilies.org/faqs/index.htm.

St. Pierre, T. (1999). *Gay and lesbian adoption: State of the issue*. Washington, DC: Human Rights Campaign.

Sullivan, A. (Ed.). (1995). *Issues in gay and lesbian adoption: Proceedings of the Fourth Annual Pierce-Warwick Adoption Symposium*. Washington, DC: Child Welfare League of America.

Sullivan, T. (1994). Obstacles to effective child welfare service with gay and lesbian youths. *Child Welfare, 73*, 291–304.

Szymanski, K. (1997, December 19). New Jersey couples win adoption rights. *New York Blade*, A1.

Tanner, A. (1996, August 16). Minister says foster children belong with "natural" families. *Edmonton Journal*, 2.

Tasker, F. L., & Golombok, S. (1997). *Growing up in a lesbian family: Effects on child development*. New York: Guilford Press.

Timmins, A. (2006, April 10). *Adoption law is up for interpretation: Gay couples' rights vary*. Retrieved April 20, 2006, from www.concordmonitor.com.

Triseliotis, J., Shireman, J., & Hundleby, M. (1999). *Adoption: Theory, policy, and practice*. London: Cassell.

Troiden, R. R. (1979). Becoming homosexual: A model of gay identity acquisition. *Psychiatry, 42*, 362–373.

Troiden, R. R. (1989). The formation of homosexual identities. In G. Herdt (Ed.), *Lesbian and gay youth* (pp. 43–74). New York: Harrington Park Press.

Turnner, C. S. (1999). *Adoption journeys: Parents tell their stories*. Ithaca, NY: McBooks Press.

Urban Institute. (2003). *Gay and lesbian families in the census: Couples with children*. Washington, DC: Author.

U.S. Census Bureau of Household and Family Statistics. (2004). *America's families and living arrangements: 2004*. Retrieved May 4, 2006, from http://www.census.gov/population/ www/socdemo/hh-fam/cps2004.html.

U.S. Department of Health and Human Services. (2006). *The AFCARS 11 report: Interim estimates for FY 2004 as of July, 2006*. Available from http://www.acf.dhhs.gov/programs/cb/stats_research/afcars/tar/report11.htm.

U.S. General Accounting Office. (2002). *Foster care: Recent legislation helps states focus on finding permanent homes for children, but long-standing barriers remain* (GAO-02-585). Washington, DC: Author.

Vanfraussen, K., Ponjaert-Kristofferson, I. & Brewaeys, A. (2002). What does it mean for youngsters to grow up in a lesbian family created by means of donar insemination? *Journal of Reproductive and Infant Psychology, 20*(4), 237-252.

Vanfraussen, K., Ponjaert-Kristofferson, I. & Brewaeys, A. (2003). Family functioning in lesbian families created by donor insemination. *American Journal of Orthopsychiatry, 73*(1), 78-90.

Verhovek, S. H. (1997, November 30). Homosexual foster parent sets off a debate in Texas. *New York Times*, A20.

Wade, T. (2005, May 10). For gay men, an attraction to a different kind of scent. *New York Times*, 1.

Wainright, J. L., & Patterson, C. J. (2006). Delinquency, victimization, and substance use among adolescents with female same-sex parents. *Journal of Family Psychology, 20*(3), 526-530.

Wainright, J., Russell, S., Patterson, C. (2004). Psychosocial adjustment, school outcomes, and romantic relationships of adolescents with same-sex parents, *Child Development, 75*(6), 1886-1898.

Walters, K. L. (1998). Negotiating conflicts in allegiances among lesbian and gays of color: Reconciling divided selves and communities. In G. P. Mallon (Ed.), *Foundations of social work practice with lesbian and gay persons* (pp. 47–76). New York: Haworth Press.

Weinberg, G. (1973). *Society and the healthy homosexual.* Garden City, NY: Doubleday.

Weston, K. (1991). *Families we choose: Gay and lesbian kinship.* New York: Columbia University Press.

Williams, M. (1997, December 24). Texas state employee challenges lesbian foster parents. *Athens Daily News,* 1.

What we think: Teen in care talk about gay foster parents. (2005, November/December). *Represent: The Voice of Youth in Care,* 8–9.

About the Author

Gerald P. Mallon, DSW, is Professor at the Hunter College School of Social Work in New York City. For more than 30 years, Dr. Mallon has been a child welfare practitioner, advocate, researcher, and educator. He is the author or editor of 18 books and numerous peer-reviewed publications in professional journals. His most recent publications from Columbia University Press are *Gay Men Choosing Parenthood* and *Child Welfare for the Twenty-First Century: A Handbook of Practices, Policies, and Programs,* co-edited with Peg Hess. Dr. Mallon earned his doctorate in social welfare from the City University of New York at Hunter College, holds an MSW from Fordham University in New York and a BSW from Dominican College in Blauvelt, New York. He is also the Executive Director of the National Resource Center for Family-Centered Practice and Permanency Planning. Dr. Mallon and his partner are parents through adoption to three young people. He can be reached via e-mail at gmallon@hunter.cuny.edu.